Allied Secret

Allied Secret

The Sinking of HMT *Rohna*

Carlton Jackson

UNIVERSITY OF OKLAHOMA PRESS
Norman

Library of Congress Cataloging-in-Publication Data

Jackson, Carlton.
  [Forgotten tragedy]
  Allied secret : the sinking of HMT *Rohna* / Carlton Jackson.
    p.   cm.
  Originally published under title: Forgotten tragedy.
  Includes bibliographical references and index.
  ISBN 0-8061-3418-6 (alk. paper)
    1. HMT *Rohna* (British troopship) 2. World War, 1939–1945—
  Naval operations, British. 3. World War, 1939–1945—
  Transportation. 4. United States. Army—Transport service.
  I. Title.

  D722.R62 J33 2002
  940.54'23—dc21
                                                        2001052222

1   2   3   4   5   6   7   8   9   10

*This book is respectfully dedicated to
the survivors of HMT Rohna
and to the memory of her victims.*

Contents

Preface to the Paperback Edition

One of the sources of pleasure (and pain sometimes, I might add) that I have received since *Allied Secret*—originally titled *Forgotten Tragedy*—was published has been the large amount of mail from survivors and from families and friends of the 1,149 soldiers lost in the sinking of the *Rohna*. They often wrote just to get things off their chest, as in the case of the Pennsylvania woman who lost her childhood sweetheart and has never seen fit to court any other male, let alone get married: "He was the one and only true love in my life, and I cannot ever forget him." Not even all the therapeutic sessions she has been through have helped her return to a normal life.

Literally dozens of sons and daughters—mostly daughters—have written to say that their fathers spoke many times of being shot out of the sea but, when pressed for details, clammed up. My book, they tell me, opened up some badly needed dialogues between and among fathers, sons, brothers, and other family members back home. One correspondent, telling a survivor about the book, said, "It is possible that [Joe] will never read it, and I think you will understand. . . . I

wasn't trying to have [him] not read the book, just wanting him to
be ready and prepared." The death of Joe's hero/big brother was a
shock, one that Joe has now "carried with him for over fifty years." A
correspondent told me, "I was reluctant just to hand them the book
without some warning. Somehow I knew it was going to be a
delayed shock even after fifty-three years." He walked up to their
home with a copy of the book in his hand, somewhat "like a military
officer might . . . in 1943." It was at this reading session that Joe and
June, his siblings, learned for the first time when and where their
brother had died. "At that point the meeting became emotional, and
we were all in tears."

"About a year ago," another correspondent told me, "[we] brought
out an old musty box containing a treasure of old clippings, a purple
heart, telegrams and other documents from the War Department.
As we went through them, I asked . . . How, Why, Where, When. . . .
We finally got a flag for him with the help of the Veterans Office
and the Post Office. These people [the victim's family] did not know
how their loved one had perished. They knew it was on a ship, in a
foreign ocean. Alone with [another child] to raise and being a very
humble Portuguese lady, she kept the grief inside her. She passed
away in 1948 or 1949."

One lady wrote to say, "My husband was on gun duty the night or
day of the disaster. [He] was in a gun turret. He was blown up in the
air and fell to the deck. He could not move [because] he was para-
lyzed. Lt. McKelvey from Bolivar, Pa., passed by Clarence. Clarence
said, 'Lt. McKelvey, please see that I get off of this ship.' Not a word
spoken, Lt. McKelvey returned with a large rope and with a struggle, lowered Clarence into the Mediterranean Sea. Clarence was
wounded. His back was fractured." He was picked up by the USS
Pioneer and put in a straight jacket, "because he went out of his
mind with pain."

Another woman wrote, "You tell of a young soldier from Kentucky being washed up on the shore; in Italy. After all of these years,
I know it doesn't matter, but I was wondering if you could get the

name of that soldier." Alas, dear lady, I cannot. This is one of many requests that have come my way since *Allied Secret* was published, and the letter only shows that this "forgotten tragedy" continues well into our own day and time.

"I first heard about it [the *Rohna*] when I was five years old," a lady related, "and as children do, I would ask over and over again long into my adult life for more details on this central event of my father's life. . . . He was awarded a Purple Heart. . . . Everything you gathered [in your book] from the men you spoke to confirmed what my father told me. . . . The only part Dad shared with us was how he was picked up by a boat that broke convoy. Dad always told us how the bombing of his ship was not covered . . . by the media."

And finally, a letter from Katy, Texas, about a young man from Iowa: "I have always wished my parents knew of the circumstances of George's death, but in a way I am glad they were not alive to read the book. I can't imagine my mother reading about the horror on that night, and knowing that was George's last experience in life. My brother, who was two years older than George, said he had a hard time reading the book, and I don't think my sister who was two years younger than George ever finished it."

A very large number of these letters came from survivors themselves. Overwhelmingly, their comments were very positive about what I had attempted in *Allied Secret*. "Whereas [the book] brought back many painful memories of that terrible night, I feel the truth is now available not only to the survivors but to all America and the world, as to what really happened. . . . I've always wondered what happened to the pilot of the plane that sunk us. I'm glad to hear that he survived the war; we were taught to kill or get killed: so were they." This letter is typical of dozens of survivors who do not hold Major Hans Dochtermann personally responsible for the tragedy. (Major Dochtermann died in 1999.)

Most of the survivors' letters were personal. Some, however, were from other observers. "The tragedy of World War II, and other wars for that matter," one reader wrote, "is the ease with which the national memory lapses." Unfortunately, that does seem to be the case. A national newsman wrote: "Reading the individual experiences . . . made me feel I was there in the oily waters with them. I felt the sense of guilt you describe that afflicts every one who has been in combat and survived toward those who did not."

The veterans of World War II are leaving us at the rate of about one thousand a day. It was most fitting, therefore, that a *Rohna* plaque was dedicated on Memorial Day, 1996, at Ft. Mitchell, Alabama. A grand military ceremony marked the occasion with Old Glory waving among the silent graves, a trooping of the color by local regiments, and stirring renditions of the National Anthem. Dignitaries from federal, state, and local governments were present, next of kin such as James Blaine and Jim Bennett spoke of their lost loved ones, and many *Rohna* survivors were on hand to give speeches.

The *Rohna* survivors continue to have annual reunions. Though the numbers attending have dwindled noticeably, recent reunions have been held in St. Louis, San Antonio, and Tucson. The 2002 reunion is scheduled for Charleston, South Carolina. A *Rohna* association has been formed, primarily through the work of John Fievet and Robert Brewer, to keep survivors, families, and other interested parties informed of various activities. One result that grew out of their labors was to get a Congressional resolution that recognized the great tragedy of the *Rohna*. Moreover, a History Channel documentary is scheduled for January 2002, marking the fifty-eighth anniversary of the *Rohna*'s sinking on November 26, 1943. The *Rohna* Association even has its own web page: <www.whidbey.net/rohna/rohna.htm>. So many things finally seem to be coming together for the *Rohna* after more than half a century of trying to get the government and public to pay any attention to it.

One of the most poignant aspects to my book is the frequency with which I receive letters and telephone calls from family members of a survivor who has just passed away. Their memory must be kept alive, for they literally saved the world from dictatorships. Long before Tom Brokaw (who featured the *Rohna* in one of his newscasts) said it, this was the "greatest generation." And as I mention in the introduction, along with Bill Moyers and tens of thousands of other grateful citizens around the country and world, the GIs of World War II still are, and will remain, my heroes.

Whatever it takes to keep what they did alive and before the attention of the nation must be accomplished. Students in oral-history programs at schools, colleges, and universities should interview as many local World War II veterans as possible. The techniques of oral history go back as far as the Greek historian Herodotus and, if taken into the proper context of other historical methods, provide a useful way of getting at explanations. The proposed World War II monument in Washington D.C. is certainly a step in the right direction; how we could have gone this long without one is incomprehensible. And last, but definitely not least, is the inclusion in high-school and college curricula of history courses dealing with U.S. involvement in World War II, the most horrendous conflict the world has ever seen.

It will be easily discernible to readers of this preface that my life has been greatly enhanced by my association with the survivors of the *Rohna*, the personnel of the *Pioneer* and other rescue vessels, and the men among the other ships in the convoy. They are a great bunch of people, and I feel ever so privileged to have met them at reunions and elsewhere—and to have told their story.

CARLTON JACKSON

Butler County, Kentucky
August 2001

Acknowledgments

This book could never have been written without the assistance of many people. First and foremost, I thank the *Rohna* survivors for writing and telephoning me with their contributions to this work— contributions that, not the least, always included their encourage- ment. My gratitude to these men knows no bounds.

Second, as everyone knows, no author would get very far in a pro- ject without good libraries and good librarians. Western Kentucky University (WKU) librarian Linda Morrissett found some much- needed materials in no time flat, for which I am grateful. The per- sonnel at the interlibrary loan department at WKU went out of their way to help me, as did the staff of the Public Records Office in Kew, London. The National Archives in Washington, D.C., pro- vided much-needed materials. My student assistant, Bobby O'Brien, was indispensable as he gathered materials, and he stayed with me to the successful completion of the project.

Here at WKU I was fortunate to receive a summer grant in 1995 and a sabbatical during the fall semester of 1995 to continue research

on this project and conclude its writing. I thank every member of
the committees who allowed me this time off. Again, I am happy to
thank WKU department chairman Richard L. Troutman for his
long-time and never-failing support of my various projects. I deeply
appreciate his help and friendship over the years. I also thank my
friends and colleagues, Professors Jack Thacker and Lowell Harri-
son, for reading the manuscript and making very good recommendations. Lester Mathews of Dora, Alabama, also read the manuscript
and made helpful comments. Ferrel Rose helped with some transla-
tions, for which I am grateful. I thank also the Southern Regional
Education Board, whose grant in aid helped fund some of the
research.

Certainly, too, I thank Hans Dochtermann, the German pilot
who is quoted in so many pages ahead. My book has been greatly
enriched by his participation. Lothar Weiss of Detmold, Germany,
and Dieter Tietz of Wetumpka, Alabama, helped in various ways.

My friend, John Fievet, and his lovely wife, Catherine, have been
mainstays in this project. More than once John has gently set me
straight on matters. I thank John and Catherine most sincerely for
their help.

I would be remiss if I did not express my gratitude to several edi-
tors at the Naval Institute Press, the only press I ever considered for
this project. Anne Collier, Jean Tyson, and Scott Belliveau kept me
"in line" on the manuscript, as did Susan Biggs. As every author
knows, one's manuscript must go through peer reviews before being
accepted for publication. To those readers, unknown to me, who certainly did keep my "nose to the grindstone," thank you ever so much.

And finally, I take pride in once more thanking my family for
their continued support of my projects: Beverly and Steve; Dan and
Grace; Hilary and Matthew; Colleen, Mega, and Katharine; and
Travis, Patrick, and Austin. And, as always, Pat.

Introduction

If ever there were a generation of destiny in the United States, it was that one born in the late 1910s through the mid-1920s. The boys became young men just as the Great Depression set in; then as soon as it began to dissipate, World War II, the deadliest conflict in the history of the world, waited for them. Thus, this was a generation conditioned and hardened by both economic privations and fierce combat against the enemy. Their contributions, both in peace and war, to the United States are manifold. In his 1994 television documentary on D-Day, Bill Moyers said that the GIs of World War II have always been his heroes. And so it is with the author of this book.

A great many of those young men conditioned by the Depression and wartime realities were on board a troopship in late November 1943 on their way to the Far East, across the Mediterranean, through the Suez Canal and Red Sea, and on into the Indian Ocean to Bombay. Tragically, they did not make it. They became the victims of one of the greatest naval disasters for the United States during World War II, second only to the sinking of the USS *Arizona* on 7 December 1941 at Pearl Harbor, which resulted in 1,103 American casualties. On the *Rohna*, a British merchant ship, 1,015 American GIs died, along with 134 British and Australian officers and Indian crewmen, bringing the total fatalities to 1,149 and making it one of history's worst maritime disasters.

Historians have asserted that the 863 men who died on the USS *Indianapolis* when it was destroyed by a Japanese ship on 30 July 1945 represented the greatest loss of American lives at sea during World War II. My study of the *Rohna* changes that perception.

There are many survivors of the *Rohna* still living today, fifty-three years after the event. It is primarily through their letters that I have been able to reconstruct that horrifying day of 26 November 1943. Most of the survivors wrote to me gladly, having desired for many years to have their story told. It has *not* been told; no history of World War II mentions the *Rohna*; not even a recent *Encyclopedia of World War II*. The destruction of the *Rohna* was shrouded in secrecy during the war because neither the British nor the American governments wanted their populace to know that the age of guided bomb warfare had arrived, and that their sons were its first victims. Still, even many years after the war, very few details of the *Rohna* were released, apparently because the American government did not wish to embarrass the British government. The time has come, however, to tell the story of the *Rohna*.

My research into the *Rohna* was greatly enhanced by my contact, after much persistence and good luck, with the German pilot who flew the plane from which the fatal bomb was fired. His name is Hans Dochtermann, and he lives in Germany. He sent me a long report, revealing his feelings about that fateful day so long ago and, quite importantly, the procedures that were followed in preparing the bomb, firing it, and finally guiding it to the *Rohna*.

There are actually no villains in my study of the *Rohna*, and many survivors of the blast feel much the same. All of the military personnel on both sides had taken an oath to fight for their respective countries. And, of course, American and British forces also were responsible for the devastating destruction of enemy ships and locales as well. The big villain in this story is War itself. And "War itself" is usually brought on by politicians, not military people. So many of the letters from *Rohna* survivors and heirs of those who were lost have made statements such as "he [the German pilot] was only doing his duty," and "we would have done the same under the same circumstances." My story, then, is about the cruelty of war, and what the brave will do in the face of almost insurmountable odds.

Receiving letters from so many men—not only *Rohna* survivors, but from those on other ships in the convoy (KMF-26) as well—I learned a lesson, probably well deserved, in irony. Two men in Kentucky, Sam Cunigan and Charles Shelton, lived only miles from each other for fifty years—and they were acquainted with one another—yet neither knew that each had been involved in the incident: Cunigan had been on the *Pioneer* and Shelton on the *Rohna*.

By far my most poignant encounter during the course of this research was with Mr. Richard Peach of Harrisburg, Pennsylvania, who is much quoted in the pages ahead. In early October 1994 I received a letter from his daughter, Vickie Todd, telling me that her father had fallen seriously ill. One of his great wishes was to see what I had written so far on the *Rohna*. I telephoned Vickie and told her that usually I do not let anyone see developing manuscripts, but that in this case I would make an exception. I mailed my incomplete manuscript (some fifty-four pages at that time) to Mr. Peach; it arrived at his home on Monday morning, 10 October. Sadly, Mr. Peach had died on Sunday night, 9 October.

Some readers might bring up the matter of memory; it has, after all, been fifty-three years since the sinking of the *Rohna*. Almost to a person, however, the survivors say that this incident is the clearest of any memory they possess, creating, as it were, a psychological fixation. It was *the* defining moment in the lives of the overwhelming majority of those who survived the destruction of the *Rohna*. Moreover, I began to notice in the letters I received a certain "sameness"; that is, the same descriptions and the same points of emphasis were being made. There could not be this much similarity in nearly a hundred letters unless all respondents were remembering it fairly much as it happened. Consequently, I am comfortable with the descriptions I have received from the survivors who are discussed in this text and deem them to be correct in all essential matters.

As pointed out before, there was much secrecy surrounding the *Rohna*. Even after the secrecy ended, documents were scattered into many different governmental repositories—a practice that exists to this very day—keeping researchers, both serious and otherwise, away from the sources.

Survivor John Fievet of Birmingham, Alabama, must be credited with carrying on a one-man crusade to get the story of the *Rohna* to the public. In April 1993 he sent a copy of a 1944 *Age Herald* story about the sinking to *Birmingham News* reporter Jay Reeves and asked him to write a "follow-up" piece. The Reeves story, picked up by the Associated Press (AP), was printed in newspapers around the country. A staff member for noted radio broadcaster Charles Osgood saw the article and persuaded Osgood to include a story about the *Rohna* in his Veterans' Day message. Because of the AP story, and to a lesser extent the Osgood broadcast, *Rohna* survivors from all over the country contacted Fievet, and soon a *Rohna* organization was formed.

There has been a movement for the past several years to establish a national memorial to those men who lost their lives in 1943 on the *Rohna* and in the sea after the explosion. Again, John Fievet must be credited with the drive behind this effort. He found James Blaine, whose brother Frank perished, and Blaine in turn filed the papers needed to make a formal request to the Department of Veterans'

Affairs for such a memorial. As a result, a *Rohna* memorial was created; it was dedicated on memorial Day 1996 at Fort Mitchell National Memorial Cemetery, Alabama. The feeling and mood of everyone connected with this story was: "It's about time."

Allied Secret

Chapter 1

A Thanksgiving to Remember

GIs, 25 November 1943: Off the Coast of Algeria

The men of the *Rohna* could see the shore of Algeria in the distance and watched with fascination as one town after another turned on its lights in anticipation of the evening. Many of the men were gathered on the shelter deck of His Majesty's Transport (HMT) *Rohna* this day for Thanksgiving dinner. The food had been bad enough on the Liberty ships that brought them across the Atlantic, through the Strait of Gibraltar, and to various staging areas in North Africa. Now they hoped for better, but they quickly discovered that such hopes were in vain.

Breakfast that morning should have been a dead giveaway. The passengers on the *Rohna* were American, the crew Indian (commonly called lascars), and the ship's officers British. For the American soldiers to expect any kind of down-home American cooking was foolish. Each GI was served a "large, greasy" sausage, about one-fourth meat and three-fourths soybean, accompanied by a plate of "slippery" fried onions, a slice of bread, and weak coffee.[1] Perhaps the British and Indians would eventually remember the significance of this day and do better for the second and last meal, which would be served late in the afternoon.

The American officers on board the *Rohna* fared much better than the enlisted men. They, along with their British counterparts, were served tea an hour or so before the Thanksgiving meal began. They had cups of hot tea, scones, bread and butter, jam, and cookies.[2] Some American officers commented on the "strict military class differences" in the British services: While they lounged in the ship's staterooms, hundreds of GIs literally were stacked on top of one another below decks. The officers also had the services of Indian "bearers" who shined their shoes, brought meals, and ran bath water for them. There was an officers' lounge on the promenade deck aft, equipped with an electric coil fireplace and cocktail bar.[3] In fact, many officers, with their lodgings on the top deck, looked forward to a long and peaceful trip to India.

When Thanksgiving dinner eventually was served, any meat the enlisted men *did* get came from a can. (According to a widespread but unfounded rumor on the ship, the officers had fresh turkey, a perception that did not help the men's morale.) Some of the troops got a bit of canned turkey; most got canned, watery chicken. A few fortunate individuals received a smattering of giblet gravy, dehydrated potatoes, "doughy" biscuits, apple sauce, and fruit cocktail. For the most part, however, the only things that did not come from a can that day were hot dogs, prepared especially for the Red Cross personnel on board.[4]

The lascars, who thought Western food was too bland to begin with (most Indian food being very spicy), were rather gleeful at the discomfort caused by the meal they served. And they did not help matters when they tried to bet several Americans—after hearing talk between British and American officers—that the ship would be "bombed tomorrow, somewhere between Algiers and Tunis." *Rohna* passenger William Quick had seen a German reconnaissance plane fly over Oran just that morning[5] (in fact, there were several) as the men boarded the troopships tied up in Oran harbor, prompting a veteran British sailor to suggest that they were in for trouble because the enemy "knows our location." A crusty old American sergeant, however, tried to put his men's minds at ease by telling them that the "Krauts" had never sunk a troopship in the Mediterranean before and that they wouldn't start today. The Allied armies, in Operation Torch the year before, had for the most part driven the Germans out of North Africa, and the coastal defenses of much of the Mediterranean were handed over to the French.[6] Many of the men and materiel from the North African Theater of War had been transferred to other locations in anticipation of the assaults on Anzio and Normandy.

But the sergeant's statement that the Germans had never sunk a troopship in the Mediterranean was, of course, untrue. On 3 November 1943 the transport *Mont Viso* from convoy KMF-30 (United *K*ingdom, *M*editerranean, *F*ast), was sunk by a U-boat; on 6 November the transport *Santa Elena* was destroyed in an air attack, as was the Dutch ship *Marnix Van St. Aldegonde* from KMF 25-A, along with an American destroyer, the USS *Beatty;* on 11 November the transport *Birchbank* and the French oilers *Nivose* and *Carlier* were sunk; on 18 November *Empire Dunstan,* another transport, was fatally attacked; and on 20 November the destroyer HMS *Jela* was sunk. All in all, these incidents proved a deadly omen for the *Rohna* of convoy KMF-26.

The 8,602-ton Rohna was built in 1926 by Hawthorn Leslie and Company in Newcastle upon Tyne for the British

India Steam Navigation Company and was registered in London. An oil-burning vessel, she measured 62 feet in width and 461 feet in length, with a top speed of slightly over 13 knots. She was 121 feet from the waterline to the top of her mast.[7] She was armed with eight 50-caliber machine guns, six 20-mm Oerlikon cannons, and two Hotchkiss and two Twin Lewis 30-caliber machine guns. These were manned by sixteen naval and two army gunners.

As early as 1931 the English governmental director of sea transport had asked the British India Steam Navigation Company for use of four of its ships "in the event of a national emergency." By 1935 this number had increased to nine, and by the outbreak of war in 1939, the total fleet (some 157 ships), including the *Rohna,* was placed at the disposal of His Majesty's government. Almost all of these ships subsequently were put into service as troop carriers.

Bespeaking her former colonial grandeur, all the *Rohna's* interdeck stairways were made of fine wood that at one time was kept highly polished. But the ship's decor had suffered as early as 1941 when she was sent as a relief ship to the besieged city of Singapore, picking up hundreds of Indian women and children and transporting them to safety.[8] By 1943 the stairways had initials and graffiti carved into them by the thousands of troops she had already carried to various war-zone destinations. For some of the war to this point, the *Rohna,* in consort with the *Varela* and *Fort Tadoussac,* had searched channels for mines and carried men and supplies between Ceylon and Bombay, India.[9] Long ago, the Indian crew quit selling chewing gum to military passengers because globs of it always were left on the decks and passageways.[10]

And unlike in days past, the *Rohna* was no longer a picture of beauty and confidence. She now was painted black, with long streaks of rust from "stem to stern"; her decks were a drab, lifeless brown. According to many men, her appearance was so brutal that they boarded with deep apprehension.[11]

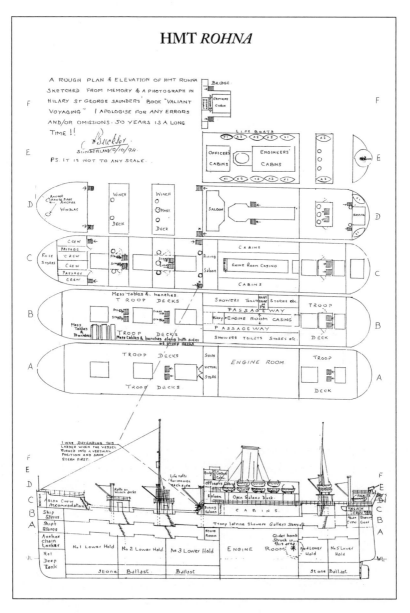

Sketch of *Rohna* deck plan.

For her previous civilian services, the *Rohna* had been outfitted for some 100 berthed passengers. On this particular voyage in November 1943, however, she had 2,193 military persons on board, most of them unberthed, plus a crew of 195. This total of 2,388[12] put the area per individual perilously close to the average for Scotch-Irish and other immigrant ships of the mid-eighteenth century (generally around two feet wide by four feet long),[13] and it was nearly the same as the ships in the Middle Passage during the unspeakable slave voyages from Africa to the West Indies. But as long as the officers would allow it, men on the *Rohna* slept in their clothes on the top deck, using duffel bags as pillows. Others slept on decks (the allotted bunk space was used up quickly), in hammocks, and even on mess hall tables after the last meal of the day had been served.

Thanksgiving meal time seemed to go along well enough—at the very least it was a welcome relief to sit up on the top decks in the brisk fresh air—until the men were served what passed for dressing: It and all of the rolls and biscuits were full of weevils.[14] There were, however, ample dollops of camel's butter to put on them. Many GIs held their noses as they passed the camel's butter to one another.[15] Everyone complained to anyone who would listen, but their NCOs always told them, "Quit your bitching. You need the protein." Wallace Mason noted that numerous cockroach colonies kept the men company at their meal. He mused later: "If it had not been for the great loss of life, that ship *should* have been sunk."[16]

The quality of the meal itself was so bad that a few men were compelled to comment fondly on the plates of creamed beef on toast, commonly called "shit on a shingle," that they frequently had been served on the voyage across the Atlantic.[17] Some soldiers pushed their Thanksgiving dinner aside in disgust and opened up cans of K rations. Many others, suffering from seasickness, did not eat at all, with the thought of *any* kind of food repelling them.

To make matters worse, the entire ship reeked of rancid engine oil, and the galley was home to several generations of rats and mice, despite the presence of the numerous cats brought on board by the crew. The *Rohna* long ago had lost any stability she once might have possessed, with the result that the creaky old vessel rolled from side to side even in calm seas. Her movements, coupled with the poor quality of the Thanksgiving meal, virtually guaranteed seasickness. Soon after dinner on the 25th—even though each person had been issued a brown paper bag for seasickness—a large contingent made their way to the heads, and soon the smell of vomit competed with the ever-present odor of oil. "The *Rohna*," said a survivor years later, "was simply not fit for human habitation."[18]

But in truth, the Thanksgiving dinner—and the way it was prepared—was not very different from the food routinely served on the *Rohna* and, presumably, all the other transports in the convoy as well. On the lower decks there were wooden tables, each of which seated twenty-four. At meal time two men took two four-gallon buckets and one flat metal pan up to the second deck, where the buckets were filled with whatever food was being served and the pans were loaded with bread. When the food was brought back to the lower decks, it was ladled out with big spoons into individual mess kits.[19] Once, John Smith ventured up to the galley and saw the food being prepared in huge steam vats. "The inside of the vats appeared clean," he said, but on the outside, "food had been allowed to boil over and dry," with an accumulation "several inches thick." It was odd seeing all this, Smith reported, "because the U.S. Navy kept things so clean."[20] James Pope equally condemned the food that day: "I had rather eat slops!"[21]

In direct contrast to the experience on the *Rohna*, not all that far away from convoy KMF-26, in Cairo, a far better Thanksgiving meal was being served. President Franklin Roosevelt and Prime Minister Winston Churchill were on their way to the Tehran Conference and were meeting with their joint chiefs of staff, with Chinese leader Chiang Kai-shek as the guest of honor. The president toasted everyone present (the only female in attendance was Churchill's daughter, Sarah) and then told the history of Thanksgiving. After dinner, a band struck up "The Marine Hymn," with the president singing along heartily. Later, he wrote in his diary: "Yesterday was a real Thanksgiving Day. The Chiangs to tea—and the British to dinner."[22] Author Paul Mayle reported Churchill as saying, "This jolly evening and the spectacle of the President carving up the turkeys stand out in my mind among the most agreeable features of the halt at Cairo." And Roosevelt told a reporter that his Thanksgiving dinner "was the most enjoyable" he had spent in a long time."[23]

Later that same evening, President Roosevelt's Thanksgiving message was broadcast over the Armed Forces Radio to all American troops throughout the world. "All of our American boys," he said, "are having turkey with all the trimmings on this special occasion." John Harding, on the *Banfora*, heard the president's report (as did all the other ships in convoy KMF-26) and said recently, "I swear every Arab between Algiers and the Suez Canal could hear all the hoots and catcalls emitting . . . that night"[24] as the convoy plied its way eastward, hoping that its escorts were up to the task of protecting them from the enemy.

KMF-26 possessed more surface escort because many convoy-supporting aircraft in the Mediterranean had been moved to the British isles in anticipation of Operation Overlord (leading up to D-Day in June 1944). Geography played a factor also. Since KMF-26 and all the other convoys came through the Mediterranean so close to the North African and French coasts, many Allied commanders believed that if these convoys were attacked at all, it would be by submarine; the Germans, they felt, would not risk being countered by the Royal Air Force (RAF).[25] Apparently this Allied belief, in part at least, caused the RAF to downgrade air support for convoys going through the Mediterranean. Well before the attack on 26 November, one skeptical British sailor had already said, "Blow up your life belts. That's the only air support we will have."[26]

The GIs on board the *Rohna* belonged primarily to the 853rd Engineer Aviation Battalion (793 men); others belonged to the 44th Portable Surgical Hospital (36 men); 31st Signal Construction Battalion (259 men); and 322nd Fighter Control Squadron (285 men). The remainder were replacements, primarily for aircraft support groups and at least one infantry unit (the 705th Infantry Replacement Battalion) for the China-Burma-India (CBI) Theater of War. Interestingly enough, however, much of the American equipment went by rail to California, then across the Pacific Ocean to various destinations.[27]

The 853rd was on its way to India to build runways for B-29s as well as hangars and other airfield structures. This battalion had been organized on 9 January 1943 in Dyersburg, Tennessee; its motto was *Honesta Quam Splendida* ("How Illustrious are Honorable Deeds"). Their first major assignment as a military unit was in the spring of 1943 when the Mississippi River flooded the Tennessee town of Lenox. The 853rd worked twelve hours a day shoring up levees and repairing those that had already broken. When one levee broke, the 853rd stopped work to rescue stranded citizens and even some livestock.

After Dyersburg, the 853rd shipped out to Brookley Field in Alabama, where they received training in camouflage and heavy construction techniques. In September they went by train to Camp Patrick Henry, near Newport News, Virginia, and in early October they boarded a Liberty ship, the *Lambert Cadwalader*, to join a convoy of seventeen ships as they crossed the Atlantic into Oran, Algeria.[28]

Landing in North Africa on 23 October 1943, many of the 853rd suffered culture shock. Instead of the romantic "One Thousand and One Nights," they were greeted with cries of "Chewing gum, Joe?" "Bon bon, Joe?" and "Hey Joe, cigarette?" In the place of "fine robes and white Arabian horses," which many of the men apparently had expected, "there were only old GI mattress covers draped around" the natives' shoulders, "and broken down mules."[29]

The 322nd, like the 853rd, had traveled in convoy in early fall 1943 across the Atlantic on the *William Rawle, Booker T. Washington, Nicholas Gilman,* and *Betty Zane.* These ships also transported the 31st Signal Heavy Construction Battalion. The trip was uneventful until the vessels reached the Strait of Gibraltar, when tension set in. One passenger saw a glow on the horizon, indicating some kind of military action.[30] Others wondered "how many German spies are watching us, and reporting our progress."[31]

But before the 322nd Fighter Control Squadron could dock, they learned that Oran was filled almost to capacity, so they disembarked at Arzew, thirty miles down the coast, and were placed in a staging area known as CP-2. For the next three weeks the outfit slept in tents, on the ground, or in sleeping bags. The climate was miserable; according to Carl Schoenacker, it was usually 100 degrees each day at noon and around 30 or 40 degrees at night. Daily temperature fluctuations of 60 to 70 degrees were not unusual. The night cold came in under the cots, and the "fleas and lice came with it!" Some GIs bought straw from local farmers to try to stay warm, while others put newspapers underneath their sleeping bags. The cold night air caused bladder problems for many of these men; thus, "bedwetting in the cold was very common."[32] Smith, corroborating much of Schoenacker's observations, was trucked to a "field of weeds" upon which tents were erected. After the second night dysentery set in, making the GIs' lives even more miserable. "We had no lights, no flashlights to find our way to the latrines that were about a block away. It was raining . . . and the soil would stick to one's shoes until you could hardly move." It is easy to understand the "confusion of 200 plus men scrambling in the pitch dark trying to get to the outdoor 20 holers in a hurry." Smith also said there was no way to take a bath except in cold water the men collected in their helmets. In Smith's opinion, the dreadful conditions in Oran and surrounding areas created such "mental and physical wrecks" that morale was nonexistent when they boarded the *Rohna;* this may have contributed to the great loss of life when the guided bomb struck.[33]

About CP-2 Ernest Horton recalled that "the nightly poker games, lit with grease supplied by the cooks in a 'C' ration can, were the high points. . . . When we left the area I'm sure all the excess rope on the tent flaps was used up for wick duty." Mason and his comrades in the 705th likewise were moved away from Oran to a tent city known as Mountain Lion.[34]

While some replacement units were on board the *Rohna,* many had already been in Algeria for some time, along with the 44th Surgical Battalion, waiting for others to arrive before shipping out any farther. Most of these American soldiers did not like the areas around Oran, except for an Algerian cafe named "Sloppy Joe's," which bore a sign that proclaimed it was the only place in North Africa where one could buy American beer.[35] They came down with physical ailments such as diarrhea, and in some instances dysentery. They also were afflicted with other maladies such as smallpox, malaria, and sandfly fever. And even those who weren't ill were for the most part restricted to quarters by their commanding officers, thus hindering fraternization with the local populace—much to the chagrin of numerous GIs looking for female company. Despite these restrictions, however, there were still a few reported cases of gonorrhea.[36]

Time, therefore, passed slowly for the GIs in Algeria. More and more, they wanted action. They played many softball games and occasionally were allowed to go on sight-seeing tours of Oran and surrounding cities. For other entertainment, however, they relied on themselves. In fact, on the night before sailing to Bombay, they staged a show in a quonset hut. One performer, a corporal named J. Freeman, played the piano and "sang as though he were a professional."[37] As it turned out, he was the nephew of entertainer Ted Lewis (whose actual name was Theodore Friedman). Corporal Freeman played and sang "I'll Be Seeing You" (which had not yet become very popular). After he finished this song, Axis Sally, a notorious Nazi propagandist, interrupted over the shortwave, announcing that the Germans knew the whereabouts of convoys in the Mediterranean and that they (the convoys) definitely would be bombed. The GIs continued with their show, and to close the festivities the corporal sang the Lord's Prayer.[38] *Rohna* survivor Eugene Breedlove later said the song "left all of us in a very quiet and thoughtful mood."[39] Corporal Freeman was one of the many on the *Rohna* to be killed.

When orders for the 322nd and 705th to board the *Rohna* finally came through, they rode in trucks to the outskirts of Oran in a blinding rain, then marched two miles with full packs until they got a glimpse of the *Rohna,* tied up at a pier in the Mediterranean. Unlike many of the 853rd (James Loper's first impression of the *Rohna* was "this has got to be the oldest ship afloat in the world, with riveted hull construction and teak wood decks"),[40] the men of the 322nd and 705th were comforted when they saw the initials HMT on the side of the ship; that meant, they believed, that the vessel was English and that they would be well cared for. "What a good deal," exclaimed one GI, while another remarked, "God it looks big and safe." It did not take long for their opinions to change.[41]

The men were marched on board the *Rohna* (many of them bent over and kissed the ground goodbye), and eventually even the officers in charge saw that she was becoming dangerously overloaded. Company "A" of the 31st boarded (two other companies of the 31st remained), but they, like dozens of their mates, were ordered off onto a sister ship, HMT *Rajula.* Thomas Conway noted that the

Rajula was tied up at the pier with the *Rohna* outboard of her. Conway and his platoon boarded the *Rajula*, crossed over her decks, and climbed on board the *Rohna*. "We had full field packs, gas masks, rifles, and bazookas, and getting down three decks with full equipment was murderous with everyone bitching all the way." But as soon as Conway and his men got settled on the *Rohna*, he and half of them were ordered back to the *Rajula*. And so the men, still with full field packs, laboriously wended their way up the ladders and once again stepped onto the *Rajula*. At the time, of course, they had no way of knowing how fortunate they were in leaving the *Rohna*.[42] Milton Garret and his shipmates on board HMT *Egra* also got a reprieve without realizing it at the time. At about 11:00 A.M. on the 26th Garret noticed that the *Rohna* and the *Egra*, for some inexplicable reason, had switched positions with each other.[43] These incidents were not the only "lucky breaks" on that voyage: Men whose names began with A–I generally were placed in the forward parts of the ship, with T–Z in the middle and J–S in the stern. The *Rohna* was hit just astern, behind the funnel.

As others boarded the *Rohna*, they saw several British officers and Indian crew members bring animals on board, prompting seamen's superstitions of doom. The officers brought dogs, and the lascars, goats; someone actually led a small horse up the gangplank. A GI from the nearby *Rajula* heard a dog howling on board the *Rohna*, reminding him of another old sailor's superstition that such an occurrence was an omen—that it would cause the ship in some way to be destroyed.[44]

Even the captain of the *Rohna*, an Australian named T. J. Murphy (who, presumably because of his love of potatoes, was affectionately nicknamed "Spud"), was accompanied by his black and white pet goat, "Neville." The goat pranced around as though it had the run of the ship—which in fact it did. One GI jokingly asked a British sailor if the goat were a mate on the *Rohna*.[45] The tar replied somewhat disgustedly that the goat, in the captain's mind at least, was

Rohna commanding officer T. J. "Spud" Murphy. *J. Buckler*

the *first* mate. In fact, there had been at least one confrontation in the past because of Neville's behavior. Apparently, it was partial to hats and once ate a passenger's cap—a passenger who just happened to be a Hussar, and very proud of his head covering. He complained to Captain Murphy, explaining that his cap's side buttons were made of gold. Unsympathetically Murphy suggested that the disaffected passenger keep a close watch on Neville for the next few days, "as he felt certain that, sound though its digestion was, the goat's stomach might be unable to assimilate the precious metal."[46]

On the evening of the 25th, on board the *Rajula,* as Conway wandered, lost, below deck and in the stern, he looked into a tiny cubicle and saw Indian women cooking food in a brazier over a coal fire. Apparently, they were the wives of the Indian crewmen. "I still can't figure out what disturbed me most," he recollected, "the women or the open fire."[47] There is no evidence that any women were on board the *Rohna*. All of the animals on board her, however, and the women on the *Rajula*, prompted the passengers to make new, dire predictions of disaster for KMF-26.

All boarding of the *Rohna* was completed in the early morning of the 25th, but even before anyone became fully settled, Captain Murphy ordered a boat drill. One soldier looked at the lifeboats and was not comforted. The skids by which life rafts would be used in case of emergency had several layers of paint on them. In all instances, the troops were told that in an emergency, the lascars would handle the lifesaving equipment. No one else, therefore, was ever instructed in these matters. (Just the year before, in 1942, there had been a report that "few officers, neither Royal nor Merchant Navy have really had much experience of boatwork at sea."[48] This message, from destroyer HMS *Zamalak*, suggested that advice therefore be sought from someone with experience in the matter. But nothing was subsequently done.) As one of the GIs remarked, "We must trust in God and the British navy to get us to India" (most had heard on the 23rd of their destination). But another GI answered this with, "Just who in hell wants to go to India?"

Finally, the *Rohna*, in company with five other transport ships— *Rajula*, *Egra*, *Banfora*, *Karoa*, and *Ranchi*—left Oran around midday on the 25th and sailed out into the Mediterranean. The *Rajula*, however, developed engine problems and turned back to port, and therefore was not involved in the subsequent attack on the convoy. All of these ships except the *Banfora*, which belonged to the French Fabre Line, were of British registry. Their immediate destination was a grouping of ships they could easily see at a distance plying eastward.

The ultimate destination for many of the soldiers, they learned, was China, to train Chinese soldiers to fight the Japanese. One

among them had had a hunch for several weeks that they would
wind up in China. Sgt. Frank W. Blaine, while stationed at Camp
Shenango, near Greenville, Pennsylvania, wrote on 28 August 1943
to his brother James that "there's a nasty rumor floating around that
2,000 of us are to be shipped to China as instructors for the Chinese
Army. How do you like that—and I can't speak one damn word
of Chinese." One of Blaine's friends argued he couldn't go to China
because he had "never learned how to eat with chopsticks." Wherever his unit went, Blaine wrote, "it's a long boat ride and I'm not
looking forward to it. I'd just as soon stay in the States myself." Blaine
subsequently was lost when the German bomb hit the *Rohna*.[49]

Ten days before the *Rohna* sailed, on 15 Novem-
ber, a major convoy formed off Gourock, Scotland, on the River
Clyde, and began its voyage. It was KMF-26. There were eighteen
ships in KMF-26, under the general command of Comm. H. D.
Wakeman-Colville, who was on the flagship, cruiser HMS *Bir-
mingham*, though later the commodore switched to HMT *Ranchi*.
The convoy's mission was to transport men and supplies to the Far
Eastern theaters.

On the way through the Atlantic, there were numerous submarine scares, one so intense that the entire convoy had to make a 180-
degree turn to avoid the Germans. As KMF-26 passed through the
Strait of Gibraltar, their radios picked up disturbing messages that
the enemy recently had carried out numerous attacks on Allied
shipping in the Mediterranean.[50]

Off the coast of Oran, convoy KMF-26 was joined by the
"Annex," the five ships of which the *Rohna* was a part. The mood
of the troops in the convoy was upbeat as they watched their new
partners come nearer to them. This addition brought the number
of ships in the convoy to twenty-four, formed in six columns, with
four to each column. The *Rohna* was assigned to position twelve,
putting her in the second position in the port column. Since she did

not have the space to maneuver as well in an attack as the ship in front (generally the easiest to target), the *Rohna* actually was more vulnerable than most. In fact, if a German flyer aimed a bomb at the first ship in the column, the chances were quite good that it would hit the second. It was not until some time later that the men on board the *Rohna* learned that this position in a convoy was always known as "Coffin Corner,"[51] presumably because so many other ships had been hit in this position.

With the Thanksgiving meal finally over, life for the men of the *Rohna* resumed its mundane course. A few men engaged the lascars in conversation, wanting to learn a bit of Hindi and inquiring about exchange rates between the dollar and the rupee.[52] Some took out books, others wrote letters home that they hoped someday would be mailed; but most resumed crap and poker games with betting that frequently reached sizeable proportions. Loper recalls, "it must have been hell on earth for the non-smokers." A "smouldering blue funk of cigarette smoke literally permeated your hair, clothing, eyelids and brows, eye balls and lungs." He watched men light their smokes from cigarettes they were about to discard, and this "did not constitute or evoke higher thoughts of mankind."[53] These poker games attracted much attention, with dozens of GIs looking on, and a lot of money was at stake in these marathon sessions. In retrospect, it is ironic that no one took advantage of the swimming and life-saving courses the Red Cross offered as part of its "Convoy College".[54]

Throughout the evening, as the men on board the *Rohna*—as well as on many of the other ships in the convoy—tried to forget the Thanksgiving dinner, a feeling of joviality spread. C. W. Finch was assigned guard duty, but he hadn't an inkling of just what he was guarding. By nightfall a mist had risen, and those on board the ships could barely see one of their own in the watery distance, let alone a German submarine.

As he stood watch, Finch suffered pangs of homesickness. And he had a feeling of expectancy: He strongly sensed that something terrible would happen on this voyage. Then there was a gnawing, indefinable dread. Maybe it was caused by all the animals brought on board by the British and lascars. He had always heard that animals on a ship presaged bad luck. He was not alone in these musings; most of his shipmates had the same mixed feelings as the convoy and their ship, HMT *Rohna,* steamed into destiny.

Later in their lives the men of the convoy also learned that for months this stretch of the Mediterranean Sea from Algeria to Tunis had been known as "Suicide Alley." Some called it the "French Flank," because of the convoy's vulnerability to attack coming from the direction of France.[55] Consequently, all kept their sights on the north and northwest, on the lookout for a German air assault from occupied France.

Chapter 2

Attack!

Germans, 25 and 26 November: Occupied France

Maj. Hans Dochtermann had sworn an oath to obey his Luftwaffe superiors, and he fulfilled his promise in 1940 by participating in the fierce air battles over France and England. He also had flown in Russia, taking part in the fighting over Stalingrad; he then joined the German attempt in early November 1943 to use guided bombs against an Allied convoy in the Atlantic. No bombs hit their intended targets, and some German pilots, including Dochtermann, believed that much work would have to be done to make the *ferngesteurten bombe* (long distance, guided bomb) program viable.[1] Of course, he had no way of knowing that barely three weeks after

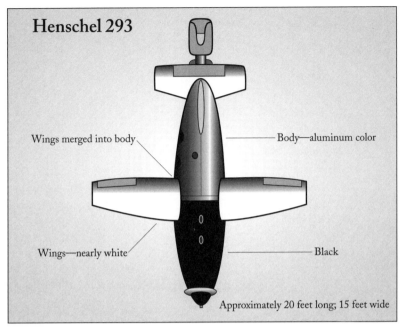

Henschel 293

Wings merged into body

Body—aluminum color

Wings—nearly white

Black

Approximately 20 feet long; 15 feet wide

Mock-up sketch of guided bomb.

this action over the Atlantic he would score the largest hit of his career—indeed, of the entire naval war in Europe.

At thirty-one in 1943, Dochtermann was a seasoned veteran of the war, but he was not yet too old to forget his childhood in the historic city of Augsburg. His father had been a self-employed textile merchant while Hans attended the *volksschule* (elementary school), where his favorite subjects were chemistry and German history, culture, and language.[2] In 1934 Dochtermann took numerous tests to get into a pilots' training school in Stettin. Of the four thousand applications, thirty-six were finally accepted for training, and of those, only sixteen from the Stettin school, including Dochtermann, were chosen to participate in the creation and development of the German Luftwaffe.[3]

From 1935 to 1939, when war broke out, Dochtermann developed his skills as a pilot and was chosen to experiment with some
new German weaponry. As early as 1937, two years before the war
began, in the eastern German city of Peenemunde, Wernher von
Braun and Col. Walter Dornberger began developing what would
become known as the V-2 rocket.[4] At roughly the same time, the
German firm of Askania and Siemens experimented with auto
pilots for unmanned flights. Each element of these newly developing technologies had to be dealt with by highly trained specialists.
Josef Schwarzmann, for example, provided the electronics, Wilfried
Hell the engineering, and Reinhard Leide and Otto Bohlmann the
aeronautics.[5] By 1939 the entire operation of building guided
bombs had been transferred to the Henschel Company, in Kassel,
and put into the capable hands of Prof. Dr. Herbert A. Wagner.
The bomb he developed—the one that destroyed HMT *Rohna*—
was the Henschel 293.[6]

Controlled tests of the developing 293 bomb
system were conducted at Karlshagen. These did not satisfy the
German authorities, according to J. R. Smith and Antony L. Kay
in *German Aircraft of the Second World War,* because weather conditions at Karlshagen prevented them from conducting high launch-
ings during the tests; yet Allied radar "made only medium and low
altitude attacks possible in later sorties."[7] In December 1940 the
Germans launched the first of literally thousands of guided bombs
that would be built by 1944. The first attempted launch—in
December 1940—was a failure, with the bomb veering off course
from its intended target and exploding. The reason, according to
I. V. Hogg in *German Secret Weapons of World War II,* was that the
right and left steering controls were not connected properly. It did
not take German scientists long to identify the problem, and they
continued apace in rocket development. During 1941 selected
Luftwaffe personnel—including Dochtermann—received special

training on indoor missile simulators. Once through the simulation, these pilots then practiced by actually firing various bombs from an aircraft and trying to guide them to selected targets.[8]

(There was at least one major American experiment with the type of guided bomb that sank the *Rohna*. Project MX 108 at Eglin Field in Florida was conducted during late 1942 and early 1943, with scientists developing five-hundred-pound "azon" and "razon"[9] guided bombs, complete with an empennage (a stabilizing tail) and autopilot. Its "mother plane" was a B-24, whose bombardier followed it down, guided by the flare in its tail, to its target. Later, a close inspection of the type of guided bomb that hit the *Rohna* showed many of the same qualities and characteristics of the bomb developed at Eglin.[10])

By 1943 Dochtermann had become a part of KG (*Kampfgeschwader*, or Bomber Unit) 40/Gruppe II, stationed at various southern parts of occupied France. A KG usually was commanded by an *oberst*, or colonel. Units within a *geschwader* (which belonged to a particular *luftflotte*, or air force) normally were divided into three (or possibly four) groups, which almost always were under the direction of a *hauptmann*, or captain. A final division was a *staffel* (of about nine planes), which best translates into English as "squadron."[11]

The night before the attack on KMF-26, Dochtermann felt certain that when he awoke the next day, orders for a strike would be waiting. And he was correct. He learned immediately from the group commander, Maj. R. Mons, that a large part of KG 40/Gruppe II would attack an Allied convoy sailing eastward through the Mediterranean. Dochtermann, along with bombardier Hans Georg Zuther (a native of Stettin who later actually guided the Hs 293 toward the *Rohna*), wireless operator Karl Rambichler (nicknamed "Rambo"), mechanic Hans Schmidt, and gunners Monfred Manhard and August Warnecke, boarded their twin-engine Heinkel 177 and joined with other members of the four staffel (some thirty-five planes altogether) that would attack.[12]

A Heinkel He 177 Greif carrying a Henschel Hs 293 guided bomb.
Luftwaffe

Dochtermann's unit of KG 40/Gruppe II took off from the German air base in Bordeaux, which had two wide concrete runways built in the form of a cross. All the planes would taxi to the cross. Then, while one plane took off on one runway to the north, another did likewise to the south. This method allowed many planes to get into the air in a short time.[13] Once airborne, through radio signals, they came together as units, reconfirmed their plans to level out at 3,500 meters, synchronized their watches—at 360 kph, it would take two hours once they reached the Mediterranean coast to get to the battle site—and flew in formation toward the south.[14]

Dochtermann himself took off at 1:55 P.M. Under each wing of his Heinkel 177 was an Hs 293 guided bomb. (The Heinkel was equipped to carry a third bomb under its fuselage, but Dochtermann did not have one on this occasion because of distance and weight factors). Once in the air, bombardier Zuther conducted a number of tests to make sure the complicated machinery of the bombs was working. The "sender," or detonator, was located in the fuselage, while radio receiving apparatuses were in the noses of each bomb. Once a bomb was released, it would be Dochtermann's job to maintain a steady course to keep it in sight; it would be Zuther's responsibility to guide the bomb to its target.[15]

Once the adrenaline of taking off abated, flight routine set in, and Dochtermann and his crew were able to reflect on a few matters. Dochtermann had been on many missions before, but as always his nerves were "torn to pieces," and things did not improve the closer the crew got to convoy KMF-26. The questions he asked himself on all sorties resurfaced: How will it be this time? What resistance will we receive? Will the Allied fighters come after us? He knew from experience that the British flyers possessed tremendous courage and were brave, persistent, and always ready to attack; he also knew if they came for him in force from the coast of North Africa, the mission might well be doomed. And they had to be prepared for attacks by French fighters. How intense would the antiaircraft fire be from the ships in the convoy and their escorts? All these concerns were intermingled with thoughts of home, and the family and friends he had left behind.[16]

GIs, 26 November: Morning

Lt. Forrest Diehl woke up early on Friday with a terrible pain in his stomach.[17] Whether it was from the food the day before or the tension of the voyage he could not say. Around mid-morning he checked in with the ship's physicians, and Drs. Wilmot Boone and Ulys Jackson decided that Diehl would need an emergency appendectomy. They could not send him off the ship at this point, since the convoy was making good time, and besides, there was no vessel to take him to shore. The doctors began to prepare him for the ordeal ahead.[18]

Corp. John Fievet and his friends sleepily made their way to the morning lifeboat drill, but for unspecified reasons the British officers were not pleased with it and promised another one at 3:30 that afternoon, although it ended up being a half hour late.[19] J. B. Gibson deemed the boat drill "not very helpful," consisting only of British officers checking the mens' lifejackets and making sure their canteens were filled with water.[20]

After the lifeboat drill, Pvt. Charles Finch managed to sleep until noon, when a loud poker party awakened him. By now the sea was getting a bit rough because force-four winds (approximately eighteen to twenty miles per hour on the Beaufort Scale) had arisen. He and his friend "Finn" tied their hammocks together to cut down on the sway and were soon asleep again. When Finch finally awoke, he climbed up on deck and looked out over the waters. The nearest ship he could see was a minesweeper—he was told that it was the USS *Pioneer*.[21]

Some of the men on the *Rohna* could hear strains of music floating over the waves from a nearby ship, the transport *Reina del Pacífico*. The chaplain was holding choir practice for the following Sunday's church services. The young men were singing Johann Sebastian Bach's "Jesu, Joy of Man's Desire" loudly and enthusiastically.[22]

When KMF-26 had entered the Strait of Gibraltar, most of its warships turned back to their own war area—in this case, the Atlantic Ocean. Apparently, however, the corvette HMS *Pelican* (which became the escort command ship) and companion corvette *Woodpecker*, the frigates HMS *Evenlode* and *Rother*, and the British destroyers *Jed* and *Brilliant* went into the Mediterranean with the convoy, because the USS *Pioneer*'s report of 26 November 1943 indicates that they took part in the action against the Germans.[23] As the convoy steamed east through the Mediterranean, an additional group of escorts arrived, made up primarily of British and American ships. The Free French were to provide air cover from their bases in North Africa, and several Royal Air Force (RAF) squadrons and a few American planes were in the area.

KMF-26 now possessed nine additional British and three American vessels. The British provided destroyers HMS *Slazak*, *Catterick*, *Miaoules*, and *Atherstone*. Accompanying these were vessels *Cleveland* and *Coventry*, the cargo ship (later turned into a specially converted rescue vessel) *Clan Campbell*, the tug *Mindful*, and the corvette HMS *Holcombe*. In addition to the *Pioneer*, the American escort vessels were the destroyers USS *Frederick C. Davis* and *Herbert C. Jones* and the minesweeper *Portent.*

26 November, 4:30 P.M.: Attack

As KMF-26 steamed eastward, all on board spent a fairly uneventful early afternoon. At around 4:30 P.M. Drs. Boone and Jackson had Lieutenant Diehl on the operating table, just getting ready to perform the emergency appendectomy. At that moment, approximately thirty German planes—mostly Dornier 217s, but also Heinkel 111s and Heinkel 177s, Focke-Wulf Kurier 90s, and Junkers 88s, coming in waves of three—swooped in on both sides of the convoy. The physicians were forced to release Diehl from the operating table. Decades later, Diehl still stands in awe of "spontaneous recoveries," because suddenly, in the face of the German attack, his abdominal pain disappeared entirely. Five years later his appendix was removed—in 1948, at Andrews Air Force Base.[24]

The attack occurred in the Bay of Bougie, about twelve miles off Cape Carbon, roughly between the Algerian towns of Aban and Bafu.[25] A radio operator on board the *Rohna*, using the "headache channel" (that is, broadcasts from the enemy that had to be simultaneously translated) at 39.5 megacycles, actually heard the Germans communicate with one another. "An alle richt voraus geleitsund," an enemy pilot reported, meaning, "The convoy is to the right and ahead of us."[26] Eyewitnesses from all the ships in KMF-26 reported that the planes came from the direction of the sun on the starboard side of the convoy and from the clouds on the port side. At first, at about four thousand feet—following the convoy's course—the Germans dropped only vertical bombs, aimed mostly at the transports in the convoy. Missing these, they then began to aim at the escorts. The Germans continued to drop free-fall bombs at the escorts; then, still in waves of three, many of the planes began to aim radio-guided bombs at the convoy itself.

The bomb was connected to the plane by a receiver that controlled a gyroscopic autopilot. The Hs 293 was powered by a Walter 109-507B liquid propellant rocket operating on hydrogen peroxide and sodium permanganate with air tanks. Producing 1,320 pounds of thrust, the bomb could travel as fast as 560 miles per hour,[27] although the one that hit the *Rohna* traveled at about 370 miles per hour.

To control the guided bomb, a bombardier operated a knüppel, or joystick. A Kehl transmitter sent the signal from the knüppel to the bomb's Strassberg Superhet radio receiver. During any attack, the mother plane did its best to stay in line with the bomb and maintain consistent speed and height.[28] Too much variance in speed, height, or direction would cause a malfunction.

According to Dochtermann, twenty-one[29] of the German planes had been armed with two guided bombs each. These planes came from the north and west and launched their bombs at the ships from some 4,000 to 6,000 yards away, with an altitude estimated by most observers as anywhere from 6,000 to 10,000 feet.

On the *Rohna*, the first sign of enemy action for many of the men below deck was the roar of the guns, not only from the *Rohna*, but from other convoy ships and escorts as well. One GI heard bullets from German planes spattering the top deck of the *Rohna*. At first he thought it was one of the sharp-clawed dogs that this day and the day before had "click clicked" across the deck, to the amusement and annoyance of those on the ship.[30] Charles Clancy could feel the shock from the explosions of the near misses and hear the clattering of shell cases hitting the deck above as the *Rohna*'s gun crews fought back.[31] The tension, however, was not too heavy at this point, and few doubted that "we could ride out this attack."[32]

John Rosseau, a radio operator on the *Rohna*, was on guard duty just below main deck, looking after a large walk-in cold storage locker used for perishable foods. He was on the port side of the *Rohna*, slightly forward from midship, near an open porthole, from which he could view the battle. He went up a ladder toward the main deck, hoping to get a better view, but was ordered back below. Rosseau's good friend, Harold Peiser from Brooklyn (who subsequently was killed), ran up to him and excitedly said that there was no one in the galley. They found large supplies of fruit, both fresh and canned, apparently destined for the officers' tables. They had not been served any fruit on board the *Rohna* and, for that matter, very little in the Oran encampment. Thus, while the battle raged outside, the two young American soldiers had their fill of peaches, apples, pineapples, and other delicacies.[33]

Captain Murphy had decided about 4:00 P.M. that he needed a shower, and he was still bathing when the attack occurred. He quickly tied a towel around his midriff and started looking for his helmet, but could not find it. Sebastion, his bearer, came running from the kitchen with a huge soup tureen, and the captain put it on and hurried to the bridge. No one laughed at him, although many were sorely tempted.[34]

When the action started on the 26th, Bruno Birsa, on board a sister ship, the *Karoa*, was below deck shaving. He heard the guns and raced, half-shaven, to the top. "You could look up," he said, "and see the German bomb-bay doors open up. There were so many 500 pound bombs falling that it looked like a long dark string hanging down."[35] Despite the danger of being hit by shell fragments from the bombs, several GIs stayed on deck and cheered each time a bomb missed a ship. Sometimes the waterspouts caused by the bombs were as high as 225 feet.

The atmosphere was almost festive to A. M. Kadis, on board the *Banfora*. "This is not really happening," he muttered to himself. "I'm watching it on a movie newsreel." The cheering, he said, was like what one would hear at a football game. "Even as the bombing around our ship ended, the excitement continued."[36]

As the klaxon sounded, Captain Murphy ordered all men on the top decks to go to their assigned quarters below. They would be in more danger from German strafing on top, he believed, than if they were in the lower decks.[37] William Wolfe owes his life, he believes, to the fact that he disobeyed the order to go below. "Our compartment was five decks below. I wasn't about to go down there."[38] He stayed on deck two and survived. Wolfe's comrade, Charles Edwards, did likewise. He was in a lounge at the ship's stern when the attack occurred. "All of a sudden the air raid siren sounded and there was an announcement on the public address system for everyone to go below. But I didn't go below. I stayed in the lounge, because I was afraid that if I went below I'd be trapped."[39] Edwards' decision to be insubordinate probably saved his life.

The *Rohna* was the only ship in the convoy—no reason was ever given—that was not flying barrage balloons, devices to entangle invading aircraft or their weapons. This condition, said Horton,[40] was the reason everyone was ordered below. Subsequently, the lack of barrage balloons was taken by numerous survivors to mean that the *Rohna* was "supposed" to be hit by the Germans.

The captain of the *Karoa* ordered all his troops to the top when the attack began, believing they would be safer from bomb hits if they were out in the open. (Each captain in the convoy apparently could use his own discretion to order troops below during an attack or keep them on deck). Fred Dettman, on board the *Karoa*, had spent a lot of time complaining about its condition. When the bomb hit the *Rohna*, however, Dettman recalled that "the old junky *Karoa* looked pretty good at that moment!"[41] Robert Loren Van Ausdall agreed with Dettman's estimation of the *Karoa*. He had been at the *Rohna*'s side, ready to board, when ordered to the *Karoa*, even though all his belongings had already been put on board the *Rohna*. "We put up a howl but all to no avail," he said. The *Karoa* master needed Van Ausdall, an Air Force captain, to help command the troops on board. "To this day," he recalls, "my foot locker and all its contents, including my wedding photo in a sterling silver frame, are on the bottom of the Mediterranean."[42] But he is not complaining about its loss: "It was my luckiest day ever."[43]

The entire convoy started a zig-zag pattern at top speed (between thirteen and eighteen knots) when the attack began, firing all guns.[44] After a time, the Germans appeared to concentrate on the ships within the convoy, as opposed to the escorts. Dochtermann has said that the *Rohna* was not deliberately picked out as a target. According to him, the Germans—at least the ones who flew the planes that day—did not even know where this convoy was headed: whether to another port in the Mediterranean or to India.[45]

Rohna's second officer, J. E. Wills, was in his cabin drinking tea when he heard the gunfire. Running back to the bridge, he saw a splash in the water off the stern of the *Coventry*, which at that time was ahead of the convoy's center, off the *Rohna*'s starboard bow. The *Coventry* sheered away to port, in the area occupied by the *Atherstone*. The second officer rang the alarm bells, "and everyone went to 'action stations.'"[46] The air raid alarm was the sound of the letter A in the International Morse Code (dit dah) on a klaxon's horn that was played over the ship's public address system.[47]

Camdon Inks stood on the top deck of the *Rohna* and suddenly saw two bombs explode in the water two hundred feet off the port bow, sending up a huge geyser. He looked up and saw fighter planes arriving on the scene—about thirty minutes after the action started—and attacking the bombers; one bomber was trailing smoke and losing altitude. Inks ran below to tell his buddies what a spectacle they were missing.[48]

Dana Hunter and a buddy went to the second deck and located the garbage disposal door. They opened it and watched the action. While German strafing bullets rat-tatted on deck, the sky was impressive, filled with "shell-bursts, tracers, and planes." Hunter watched as a German bomber attacked a minesweeper (probably the *Pioneer*). "He [the Dornier] missed but they [gunners on the minesweeper] didn't, and he went down into the sea with a huge splash and explosion."[49]

Lt. R. G. Hand was playing dice when the attack occurred and at first thought it was the routine checking of guns that the *Rohna* and all her sister ships went through every day. He finally was convinced, however, that "this is for real," so he grabbed his dice, stuck his winnings in his shirt pocket, and ran for the nearest porthole. Since he was an officer, Hand was permitted on deck, where he saw "aerial torpedoes" all around him.[50]

Richard Phythian wanted to get to one of the antiaircraft guns on board the *Rohna* and fire at the three German aircraft diving after another ship in the convoy. Before he could carry out his plan, however, an officer ordered him below deck. He and his buddies sat at a long table in the enlisted mens' dining room, where he read his GI Bible and prayed that he be spared the sacrifice of life he knew, almost instinctively, that this Nazi attack would bring about. Dr. Boone, who had been preparing to perform the emergency appendectomy on Diehl when the attack began, *did* pick up a 45-caliber pistol and fire point-blank at the intruders, to no avail. Of course, with the dive bombers at two hundred to five hundred feet, the physician's shots were more symbolic than real.[51]

When those men who obeyed Captain Murphy's order to go below did so, the first thing they did was rush, pushing and shoving, to look out the portholes in their quarters: They wanted to see the action. Horton saw a plane drop in flames and a bomb narrowly miss the USS *Pioneer*.[52] Gibson watched the escorts race up and down alongside the convoy, firing all their weapons.[53] Bill Quick could see ships' tracer shells reaching up to the intruding aircraft; one bomb came so close to the *Rohna* that he saw paint chips fall from the overhead and bulkheads.[54] Many ships in the convoy, such as the cruiser *Columbo*, fired erratically at the intruders, undoubtedly because of the frequent changes of targets and the drastic alteration of their courses to avoid being hit.

Chaplain C. Albertus Hewitt decided to leave the deck and go below to comfort the men. As he strode forward, "my eyes sought to pierce the haze of blue-gray tobacco smoke which further accentuated the feeling of confinement." In one passage he met a crew member who flattened himself against the bulkhead to let the clergyman through. "He shot me a wan smile, and I could see that his eyes were sick with fear." One GI spoke to the chaplain:

"Hello, Chaplain, how is it going?"
"Some of them [enemy planes] have been shot down,"
    answered the chaplain.
"Maybe we better have our service now instead of Sunday,"
    one man suggested in, as Hewitt noted,
    "a voice that hung between a jest and a prayer."

Hewitt reported further: "We were like men standing at our own grave, or, more exactly, in our own grave. The feeling of futility was awful. There was no place to go, nothing to do. . . . Fear was present, but it was made captive by courage. Each man was passively playing the role of a hero."[55]

Most of the men could only *hear* the battle, not *see* it. For one thing, since it was getting so late in the day and close to blackout time, lascars came through the decks closing all the portholes, even while the German attack was in full progress. For another, there simply weren't enough portholes for everyone to look through. Finch noted that "our ship was firing everything she had. . . . The noise was something out of this world. . . . [T]he ship would shudder and shake just [as though] we had been hit." Finch made his way to the head to join a long line of other GIs waiting to look at the aerial dogfights through a small porthole. A short distance from the head he found a sergeant at the top of a crowded stairway, trying to keep the men below (who quickly realized the futility of Captain Murphy's orders) from going up and those above (who were still trying to obey those orders) from coming down. In an understatement, Finch remarked, "It was a nightmare."[56]

Even though the ships in KMF-26 had noted the earlier German reconnaissance planes, there had been no immediate warning of an enemy attack. The escort commanders, at least, had received no word on who would be the senior escorts, or even who the overall commander of the convoy was. Was it still Commodore Wakeman-Colville? If so, just where was he? One report said he was on board HMT *Ranchi;*[57] another said he was on HMS *Slazak.* Furthermore, no radio code calls were assigned to any of the escorts, making their job more difficult once action did begin. According to widespread American belief, the British officials considered these kinds of communication information between each other to be "minor" and therefore not worthy of being shared.

To combat the bombs, Allied escorts knew they could use electronic jamming. Radio operators on board escort vessels determined that the radio-guided bombs' frequencies were 48.5, 49.0, 49.75, and 50.0 megacycles. At least six of the twenty-four guided bombs were rendered useless through this kind of jamming.

The second ploy was to put up a thick smoke screen. Many ships in the convoy had a chloral sulfonic acid smoke-making device. Its cylindrical drum was seven feet long and three feet, six inches in diameter. Situated over the stern of the ship, it was operated by air pressure at one hundred pounds per square inch. The total weight of the unit was about eight tons. If the smoke screens could be generated at night or near night "quickly and effectively," they would be a valuable defense. In some instances in the past, however, the smoke screening vessels had used white smoke, and the screened vessels had used black, which easily could be seen by enemy aircraft through the white smoke. In such a case, the pilot of an enemy aircraft would be able at least to approximate the location of the screened ship.[58] All ships in KMF-26, therefore, were ordered to "make smoke with whatever means at their disposal," and they did—the only stipulation being that they make the smoke of the *same kind*—black on this occasion—and consistently throughout the convoy.

American and British directives believed that the best way of avoiding being hit by an Hs 293 was to shoot it down—although many gunners tended to shoot at the aircraft that fired the bomb. Were these tactics to fail, a "drastic alteration of course" would be called for. In fact, it was discovered by convoy captains that changing a ship's course directly toward an incoming plane that was expected to release a bomb was one of the better tactics. This maneuver, according to widespread opinion, saved the *Colombo*. Two other ships, the *Ranchi* and the seriously overcrowded *Orion*, had near misses. In fact, a guided bomb *did* hit a cargo crane on the *Ranchi*, resulting in one fatality.[59] Guided bombs flew directly over both ships and exploded on impact with the water. (It is entirely likely that the guided bomb that just missed the *Orion*—the largest ship in KMF-26—was fired from Dochtermann's plane, since he spoke of picking out the biggest ship in the convoy.) Also, maneuvering at flank speed probably had much to do with the lack of success.

Gunners from the various escort and convoy ships kept up such a barrage of ack-ack fire that it created a flak barrier, forcing the Germans to peel off and come in several times, costing them time and fuel. Harrell Jones, gun captain on board the *Pioneer*, used 10-, 12-, and 15-fuse settings (meaning that shells would explode in the aircrafts' paths every ten, twelve, and fifteen seconds), helping to intensify the flak. "This broke their formation," Jones said, and made it increasingly difficult for them to home in on their targets.[60] From the nearby *Banfora*, it appeared that the *Pioneer* was on fire because she was throwing up so much flak.[61]

According to Dochtermann, "The flak laid a black carpet in the air of explosive clouds," impeding the plans of attacking the convoy.[62] He noted that several German aircraft were destroyed, whether through RAF action or flak, he could not say. He knew that the flight crews aboard these German bombers were outfitted with parachutes, but they were flying so low that they could not activate them, and he watched with dread and fascination as their planes made impact with the water, "sending up high fountains" in the Mediterranean. He knew that on each of these occasions some of his comrades were lost. To better see all of the action, Dochtermann flew to the south, over the port of Bougie, where an Allied aircraft carrier, which he did not name, lay at anchor. The great ship fired at him with all its barrels, but he dodged to the east, back toward the direction of the convoy.[63] English gunner John Rourke was manning a Bofors in the Bougie harbor. "This 177 Heinkel," he noted, "seemed to break away from the raiding party." Rourke got the plane in his sights and elevated his gun, preparing to fire. At that moment, however, his commanders telephoned and ordered him *not* to engage the plane. It was being followed, he was told, by Spitfires, and the RAF wanted the "kill."[64] Set upon by several British fighter planes, Dochtermann beat a hasty retreat out over the Kabylie Mountains—which were a mile out in the Mediterranean.

Bombardier Zuther had some 7.92-mm MG 81 guns at his disposal, but they had always proven so ineffective that the Germans called them "garden hoses." In addition to these, the Heinkel 177's weaponry consisted of two 20-mm MG 151s, one in the hull at the bottom of the plane toward the front, another toward the back, both operated by the aircraft mechanics. There were two fully rotatable 13-mm MG 131s operated by "Rambo," the radio operator, and there was another MG 131 at the top side of the fuselage, remotely controlled and fully rotatable at 360 degrees. Finally, there was an MG 151 in the tail turret operated by the rear gunner. Dochtermann reported later that these men "gave" as well as they "got."[65]

When the attack started at 4:30 P.M., four French Spitfires from the Northwest African Coastal Air Force (NACAF) were over the convoy on routine patrol, as were four RAF Beaufighters north of the convoy in the vicinity of the Balearic Islands. A Wellington provided antisubmarine support. As the fighting continued, eight more RAF Spitfires, six more Beaufighters, and four RAF P-39s from bases in Bone, Le Sabala in Algiers, and Protville, near Tunis, joined the action. Sam Cunigan noticed one or two American planes from, he surmised, either Algiers or Bizerte.[66] The RAF was put off by the timing of the attack, which came at 4:30 P.M. instead of two hours later, when dusk would be gathering, thus making it difficult for the convoy's escort gunners to sight enemy aircraft. One routine British patrol, led by Flt. Lt. R. Charles, "took off to intercept an enemy strike force believed to be flying south to attack a large convoy off the coast at last light. Unfortunately, as the enemy timed their attack [at 4:30 P.M. instead of 6:30 P.M.] to commence two hours earlier than expected, our aircraft made no contacts with enemy aircraft."[67] In other words, the action had ended by the time the major striking force of the RAF arrived on the scene.

Nonetheless, Allied fighters gave a good account of themselves as KMF-26 was being attacked. An RAF pilot reported: "Lost a visual on one aircraft, but picked up a straggler identified as a Junkers 88, and a Heinkel 177 which caught fire and went into the sea. Bursts of guns got another Heinkel 177. . . . Two other Heinkel 177s damaged."[68] Chief Wrnt. Ofc. William McCullough, on board the *Banfora,* saw two British fighters attack the German formation. One Junkers 88 was hit and fell into the sea, causing the British pilot to go into a "victory roll" right over KMF-26. His plane was hit by gunfire from one of the convoy's escorts and fell into the sea. The other fighter "left the area, and was not seen again."[69]

Altogether, in terms of the total aircraft involved in the attack on KMF-26, the Allies reported two planes missing, but according to William Green in *War Planes of the Third Reich,* of the fourteen Heinkel 177s, four were destroyed outright, and three more had to be discarded after landing back in France. Thus, fifty percent of the Germans' Hs 293 carrying force was destroyed in the attack on KMF-26; and KG 40's commander, Major Mons, was killed. In fact, the attack on KMF-26 caused the Germans to change their tactics for future forays. As Green reports: "The heavy losses sustained indicated that daylight attacks against convoys with the

Henschel 293 were impracticable, and it was concluded that attacks on shipping would have to be carried out at night."[70] Nonetheless, the Henschels were efficient enough to disturb all those who saw them, if for no other reason than that these men witnessed the introduction of a new, dreadful weapon of war. A report from the *Colombo* asserted: "It must be admitted that the gliders ran unpleasantly well. Of all the forms of attack I've seen, I like the gliders least. One sees them for so long and feels helpless."[71] Some British sailors began calling the guided bombs "flying angels," presumably because they could send one to heaven in a hurry.[72]

Allied experience had shown that there were three kinds of guided bomb attacks. In the first, the plane (almost always a Heinkel 177) ran in on the target outside surface gun range. As the plane turned away, the bomb came in on a long, straight glide. The second method was the side attack, in which the plane turned first toward the target and, just as it released its bomb, veered sharply away, while the bomb curved in toward the target. The third type of attack, used by Dochtermann, was the banking turn. Here the plane ran parallel to the convoy and then in front of it. When the bomb was released, the pilot turned sharply away to the left—some thirty degrees away from the longitudinal axis of the target ship—while the Hs 293 made a long, somewhat erratic curve, first for a short distance to the left itself—toward the mother plane—but then took a wide swing to the right and wound up in almost the opposite direction of its "parent."

Altogether, there were two major waves of German attacks. The first one lasted from 4:30 P.M. to about 4:45, the second from about 4:50 to 5:00. Everyone on the convoy's ships watched with relief as the last of the Germans disappeared. A few of the men were allowed back out on deck. Captain Murphy found time to dress and returned to the bridge in full battle gear, with the exception of his helmet, which he still couldn't find. He stood on

38

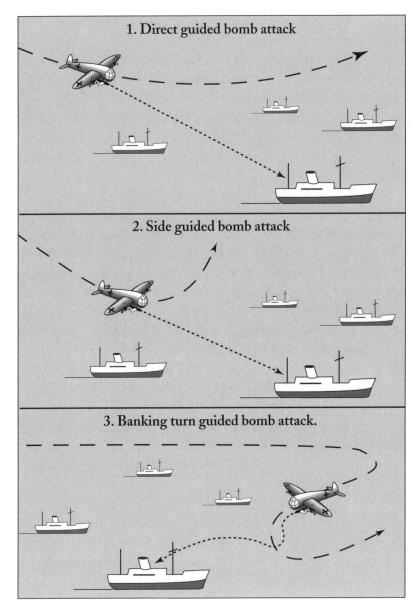

1. Direct guided bomb attack

2. Side guided bomb attack

3. Banking turn guided bomb attack.

Sketch of the three different ways guided bombs were fired. Major Dochtermann used number 3.

the bridge, soup tureen on his head, and calmly smoked his pipe, much to the muted amusement of those around him. Third Ofc. John Buckler, who had managed to hold the *Rohna* on a steady course as she was jolted by her own firepower during the attack, continued at the helm.

Meanwhile, Dochtermann was annoyed that he had had to fly so high to avoid the flak that any shot he aimed at the convoy could not possibly hit. He sharply ordered bombardier Zuther to prepare the Hs 293 for firing.[73] His target: the largest ship in the convoy, possibly the *Orion*. The Germans had a rule of thumb that each lifeboat they could see strapped alongside an Allied ship accounted for one thousand tons.[74] Thus, they simply looked for the ship with the most lifeboats. Using this rule of thumb, Dochtermann thought he was dealing with a ship of about twenty thousand tons displacement, which clearly would have been more like the *Orion* than the *Rohna*. It is entirely possible that the Hs 293, presumably initially intended for the *Orion*, which was off to the *Rohna*'s starboard, changed its course in flight and headed toward the *Rohna* instead.

As the men on board the convoy ships and escorts celebrated and enjoyed the lull, a few looked up and saw a plane returning. In the distance, it appeared to be German, and the trained eye could tell that it was a Heinkel 177.

Chapter 3

The Guided Bomb

Germans, 26 November: 5:13 P.M.

Dochtermann liked to do things by the book,
strictly adhering to Luftwaffe procedures. Even
while he and his colleagues studied missiles
in flight school, taking such courses as Flying at
Sea, they were issued a handbook, which they
irreverently referred to as "the prayer-book for
the 177ers,"[1] instructing them on how to spot
targets, how to determine the precise moment of
firing an Hs 293, how to guide it in the ninety
seconds it would take to get to its target, and
how to avoid enemy air attacks.

In the chaos surrounding the attack on
KMF-26, however, organizational procedures
frequently gave way to improvisation. Improb-
able as it may have seemed, the heavy flak bar-

rier worked to Dochtermann's temporary advantage. No fighter planes were deliberately going to fly through the deadly black carpet of explosives. This situation gave Dochtermann momentary relief from the attentions of the Spitfires and Beaufighters. Then he found a heavy cloud cover, which gave him additional opportunities to ready his attack. "As through a telescope," he recalled later, he had to keep one eye on the targets below, "read the range," and coordinate this information with bombardier Zuther. With the other eye, he watched the altimeter, variometer (a device to measure electrical circuitry), and gyrocompass to make sure the proper altitude and course were maintained.[2]

While running parallel to the convoy's course, Dochtermann's plane flew directly over a destroyer, probably the *Atherstone,* which opened fire on him without results. Then Dochtermann turned thirty degrees away from the convoy and released the bomb, simultaneously setting the second hand on the stopwatch mounted on the steering column. After the weapon fell some one hundred meters, Dochtermann saw its rocket motors ignite and the bomb increase speed. The bomb was now out in front of the plane, and Zuther used his knüppel to keep the red-hot flare he could see from the tail on a path straight for the *Rohna.* As Dochtermann began to turn the plane, Zuther had nearly to lie on his back to see the bomb and continue steering it.[3] In a television documentary entitled *Guided Bomb* (1993), noted aviation historian Dr. Alfred Price explained that the Hs 293 operated by a system known as "guidance command to line of sight." Zuther's job was to superimpose the flare onto the target and guide it with his knüppel down the line of sight until impact.[4]

After a few seconds Dochtermann could not see the bomb at all, since his seat was on the left side of the cockpit and the bomb was off to his right. His job at this moment, however, was to concentrate exclusively on his flight instruments to keep the plane flying in a way—at a height of about 2,500 meters (8,000 feet)—that would be most beneficial to Zuther.[5] After sixty seconds, Dochtermann had little hope of a score, and at ninety seconds he had given up. Precisely ninety-two seconds after the Hs 293 left the plane, there was a loud, resounding, and highly enthusiastic shout over the craft-to-craft radios from the personnel of five different planes in Dochtermann's squadron that were still in the area. Almost every one of the German airmen shouted "Volltreffer mittschiffs!" or "Direct hit midships!" Dochtermann's tailgunner, Warnecke, exclaimed that "Just now the captain of the ship has taken his pipe from out of his mouth."[6] Just what this phrase meant is unclear. Was it an inside joke among the flight personnel, and simply a bizarre coincidence? After all, Captain Murphy was known to be very fond of his pipe.

After Warnecke's exultation, he fished his harmonica out of his flight bag and began playing a song familiar to many German soldiers during World War II: "Denn wir fahren, denn wir fahren, denn wir fahren gegen Engeland" ("Because we're traveling, because we're traveling, because we're traveling toward England.")[7]

Immediately after his hit on the *Rohna*, Dochtermann's plane was attacked by two fighters. He pushed in his throttles and, at 550 kilometers per hour, went into a steep nosedive. At this speed the wind pressure was so great that it broke out a locked window in the cockpit and filled the entire plane with "fresh sea air." He leveled out at a few meters above the water and tried flying on an eastward course to get himself out of the zone of fire, only to find that the two Allied planes were still after him. The ships in the convoy were firing at him as well, apparently hoping he would get near enough to the water so that his propellers would be caught in one of the crests that began building up as twilight set in. The foaming whitecaps, however, gave Dochtermann some advantage. Planes from above could not see him as easily as if he had been flying at a high altitude through open space. (One of Dochtermann's colleagues,

Capt. Fritz Hoppe, raced so fast down toward the convoy that both wing ends bent upwards as they were caught just above the water. He survived.)[8]

Instead of crashing into the waves, however, Dochtermann found what he deemed a miracle. Some 10 to 15 kilometers in front of him and to the north, he noted a very thick cloud bank—perhaps it was fog—at 250 meters (about a quarter mile). He knew that if he could get into this camouflage he would no longer be bothered by Allied hunters or convoy antiaircraft fire. Again, he went to full throttle up from the waves and soon disappeared into the cloud cover. Unfortunately for him, it was not as spread out as he had hoped, and soon he was back into free space. There were no hostile aircraft around him, however, and he was far enough away now from the convoy—although he could still see its ships shooting at him—not to worry anymore about its firepower. Dochtermann immediately set his sights on getting back to his home base in southern France.[9]

GIs, 26 November: 5:15–5:30 P.M.

To a Beaufighter pilot, the Heinkel appeared to have taken on two additional engines. The Hs 293s were attached to the wings' bottoms; each projected two to three feet in front of a wing and about four feet behind it. Since the wing width of a Heinkel was thirteen feet, this meant the Hs 293's length was about twenty feet, with an estimated weight of between 1,000 and 2,000 pounds. It was designed to be shot from a moderately high altitude (6,000 to 10,000 feet) and penetrate either lightly armored or unarmored ships.[10] Conversely, the Hs 293's "sister" rocket, the 1400 X, or Fritz X, was specifically intended for armor-plated ships and was fired from a higher altitude, generally around 20,000 feet. Fritz X rockets a year or so previously had hit the British battleships *Warspite* and *Winchelsea* but had not sunk them.[11] A Fritz X was used, however, to destroy the Italian battleship *Roma*—often confused with the *Rohna*—after she had surrendered to the Allies and was being towed into a port.

Dochtermann's Heinkel carried two bombs, both of which may have been fired. Paul Different was on board the *Banfora,* one of the *Rohna*'s sister ships, and was confident that the plane fired two bombs,[12] one of which headed straight for the *Banfora.* A wing was shot off this initial bomb, causing it to veer into the sea, but not before striking the radio antenna that stretched between the forward and aft masts, scattering large pieces of debris on the *Banfora*'s deck.[13] Different said that the second bomb, however, escaped damage from antiaircraft fire and slammed directly into the *Rohna.*

Dochtermann and his Heinkel came in from the north at about eight thousand feet, flying astern and parallel to the convoy's course. Many on the ships and in the air saw the Heinkel—around six thousand yards away—go into a steep dive and suddenly apparently burst into flames, accompanied by a lot of smoke. Some on the surface cheered, because they thought the Heinkel had been hit.

Almost instantaneously, however, they observed a small "bomber," which appeared to be shaped "like a black cigar," slightly behind the enemy plane. In a few seconds, when its first rocket fired, this "bomber" overtook the Heinkel and passed about thirty feet below its line of flight and in front of it. Two more rocket firings (each lasting, said Wrnt. Ofc. F. B. Forge, from one-half to one second and each following in rapid succession) accelerated the bomb and put it on course.[14] Even after all the rockets were expended, radio-control devices from the plane continued to keep the bomb on course. The "bomber" then began to fall at an angle of sixty degrees from the horizontal, and once more there was another Allied celebration, because they believed this object had been destroyed.

The bomb kept a downward spiral, its nose red from heat and its tail spewing a thick line of black smoke. The *Rohna*'s port Oerlikons opened fire on the intruder, but all shots missed. To many British, the bomb appeared to be a "large paravane" (a device to support and divert a wire cable, which may be equipped with cutters, towed by a ship sweeping for moored mines). The object had a cylindrical tail, with four to six Venturi tubes (controlling the rate of downward speed) visible.[15]

Some in the convoy ships below thought it resembled a P-39 on a suicide mission, while British Lt. C. Benner and U.S. Lt. Col. Alexander Frolich, commander of the 853rd, surmised that it was a burning enemy fighter plane that had been hit.[16] Hunter, however, believed it to be a tiny plane with stubby wings and no propeller.[17] Lt. Robert Brewer, looking through a porthole, "saw little wings on its side so at first I thought it was a small fighter diving in toward us."[18]

Captain Murphy, standing on the port side, also saw the bomb. He pushed back his soup tureen and scratched his head. As Fievet declared later, Captain Murphy did not know "that he was seeing history in the making."[19] Red Cross worker Jeff Sparks was below deck and saw the bomb through a porthole. "What the devil is that?" he exclaimed. Then he ran away quickly, hoping to get to the other side of the ship before impact.[20]

When the bomb neared the surface—some twenty to thirty feet above the waterline—it veered off on a wide swing to port; many thought it was going out to sea and were gladdened at the prospect. At the same time, the bomb's mother plane banked toward the convoy and made a circle, again directly over the *Atherstone*. The latter fired twelve four-gun salvos at the plane, as well as Oerlikons at the bomb.

After the bomb veered leftward, it straightened out and seemed to head straight for the *Rohna*; a few of the men on board speculated that it was zeroing in on some kind of homing device on the ship. It seemed to shimmy up and down as it headed for the *Rohna*, as if it were going through a series of hills and troughs, traveling at approximately 370 miles per hour. Many men saw that a hit was imminent and jumped backward to avoid impact. Others hit the deck, hoping to save themselves from a head-on collision. For an instant it appeared that the bomb would hit the ship in the stern or even miss altogether and go out to sea. It hit astern of the single funnel in the area of the engine room, however, some fifteen feet above the waterline, causing a loss of all lights, communications, and water pressure. As one person said later, the *Rohna* was "dead in the water,"[21] with her engine room on fire and propellers inoperative. Nearby, on decks six and seven, the troops of the 853rd were lodged. All but a few of the men working in the kitchen were killed instantly.

The explosion ripped through the engine room, stopping the propeller shaft immediately and sending up smoke nearly three times the height of the ship's mast. All the way from the funnel aft, the *Rohna* was in flames. The explosion was so powerful that it went upward through the starboard promenade deck and blew some of the ship's superstructure, including a stack, in all directions, killing several of the gun crew on the top deck. A report from the nearby *Arundel Castle* noted that the base of the resulting smoke cloud occupied at least one-third of the ship. About twenty minutes later a "sheet of flame leapt to a steady height of about 100 feet, testifying to the large size—it weighed some 1,500 pounds—and power of the bomb."[22]

It is impossible to say just how many immediate casualties resulted from the explosion. A fair estimate would be three hundred killed, one hundred wounded. In one of the lower holds a group of engineers was sealed inside with no chance of escape. Others were killed by fire, explosions, and falling debris.

GIs: 5:16–5:30 P.M.

Thud. This is the word most survivors used to describe the impact of the Hs 293 into the lightly plated port side of the *Rohna* on that gray November day.[23] There was no alarm, said Inks, and no instructions.[24] None was needed: "We knew we had been hit." To Clarence Bailey it was a "tremendous explosion" that rocked the ship "like a vehicle that was hit with a train."[25]

The bomb went through the port side of the *Rohna* astern of the funnel; seconds later, as it slanted at about forty-five degrees through the interior of the ship, it exploded, because of its delayed-fuse settings, and opened a sizable hole on the starboard side right at water level. The resulting two huge holes caused the *Rohna* immediately to list to starboard. According to Kadis, on the *Banfora,* the portside hole was about seventy-five feet square. "You could see straight through the ship." Looking from the deck of his ship, he saw many ropes coming down from the *Rohna*'s deck. Some ropes were too short to reach the water, but their ends "were silhouetted in the gaping hole." The men bumped into one another, and frequently a soldier jumping from the top deck would fly by them. It was, Kadis affirms, "the most horrible sight I have ever seen."[26] McCullough, also on the *Banfora,* was certain he saw Captain Murphy standing on the *Rohna*'s deck (he was bareheaded, apparently having shed his soup tureen). McCullough assumed he was the captain of the ship because he kept gesticulating, obviously giving orders to abandon ship. McCullough was close enough to see the braids on Captain Murphy's sleeves.[27]

Nearby, LeRoy E. Rogers, commanding officer of the *Pioneer,* looked at the two holes in the *Rohna:* "I'll never forget being able to look completely through the ship and readily see other ship activity on the other side. There was no way that ship could have been kept afloat. Even if it could, the result would have been just one big cinder." Through the flames and smoke, Commander Rogers noted, "we began to see people jumping over the side to swim away, toward us."[28]

At the moment of impact, Breedlove was standing guard duty on the *Rohna,* keeping watch over a lone soldier who had had too much to drink of (apparently) smuggled liquor and was in the brig

Carl Schoenacker after the *Rohna* sinking.

to sober up. When the hit occurred, both prisoner and guard were released to return to their outfits. Breedlove recalled that "the soldiers didn't seem to panic," but "you could hear the screams of the men who were injured."[29] Edwards was knocked down a flight of wooden stairs. "I was out for five or 10 minutes, and when I woke up it was pitch black and the ship was rocking back and forth."[30] Loper stated, "I vividly recall a force lifting me into the . . . [overhead], and blacking out." When he regained consciousness, his hair and clothes were on fire. "I was flat on my back in total darkness and people were running and stepping on my legs, stomach, and chest."

He began walking toward where he believed there was a stairway, but he never got there. He fell through a hatch that had been considerably widened by the blast and was knocked unconscious for a second time. He found himself lying on "steam drenched" barracks bags. All around him were dead men, and his left leg was seriously swollen. "It was like a movie," he remembered later. "This cannot be."[31]

Schoenacker's playing cards were scattered in all directions by a strong draft. "I cannot call it wind because wind has direction." He hunted for his cards in the dark, then said to himself, "You fool, this is serious; you are not going to use those again."[32] Second Officer Wills noted that the bomb did not cause a loud explosion; in fact, the "near-misses," detonating harmlessly out in the sea, had been louder. Wills and his colleagues spoke of "implosions," of having everything on the ship pushed together rather than pulled apart. Other reports spoke of "terrific concussions." [33] Louis Rees was in a lower deck when the bomb hit, and "it seemed to suck all the air out, which made it difficult to breathe for a few seconds."[34]

Schoenacker's buddy, Reed, had gone to a porthole in the nearby head.[35] He, along with everyone else there, was never seen again. Charles Bauer had just gone broke in a poker game and decided to take a shower. "I was carrying a towel and a cake of soap. I only had on a pair of shorts." All of his buddies in that poker game were lost.[36]

Other poker players, however, said Richard Peach, apparently were nonchalant about the whole thing. Despite the sparks, cracking sounds, and lights going out, several men lit matches to see what cards they were holding. Peach, four flights of stairs from the top deck, gazed upwards, and one of his buddies asked him, "Peach, what are you doing? Checking those rafters to see how firm they are?" Peach somberly replied, "No, I'm saying a prayer." He walked over to a stairway that was still intact and stood there. A corporal told him, "I wouldn't stand there if I were you; if that hatch cover comes crashing down, you'll be under it." Peach walked away right at the point when the cover crashed into his compartment. He

Schoenacker's buddy, William Reed, lost
on the *Rohna*.

undoubtedly would have perished had it not been for the corporal's
prescience. Many of Peach's comrades were not so lucky: They were
hit by hatch covers falling from decks above them.[37]

There was, of course, trouble all over the *Rohna*, but none so pronounced as on the lower decks. But even here there was still some
joviality; perhaps this was an attribute of the ever-present optimism
of youth. One young man, a devoted fan of Erle Stanley Gardner's
Perry Mason novels, told everyone to relax: "Perry Mason says it'll
be over in fifteen minutes."[38] He did not comfort too many people
with this assertion. Other young men made jokes, even at this grave
hour, about how many of their comrades, right at the moment when
the bomb hit, reached into their pockets and pulled out condoms

to protect watches, rings, wads of cash, cigarettes, and other valuables from seawater.[39]

Elsewhere on the ship, Brewer had gone into a lower-deck passageway at the height of the attack and found a major and captain talking over the situation. The major was calm, he recalled, but the captain was nervous. As the conversation turned to various types of aircraft used in the war, there was a sudden "Poof!" that threw the men across the passageway against the opposite bulkhead. In Brewer's words, "There was nothing but darkness and the acrid smell of gun powder mixed with steam that was hot on our faces and hands as we tried to gather our wits. . . . I reached out and found a man's waist. . . . I grabbed his belt and felt someone grab onto mine. . . . We began inching our way forward in the darkness and steam toward a stairway we knew to be near the dining room."[40]

Having just left the porthole in the head, Finch was knocked to the deck and slid until stopped by an overturned bunk. Helmets, footlockers, paperback books, half-written letters, magazines, and prostrate GIs, both dead and wounded, pitched toward him, and he dodged them as best he could. What he remembered most, however, were the huge, jagged splinters that undoubtedly had come from the *Rohna*'s numerous wooden stairways, railings, and heavy overhead beams. As he listened to comrades calling for help (one screamed over and over, "We're going to be killed!" until someone said, "Shut up!"), Finch felt his back and found it wet with blood. Probably from the splinters, he surmised, before he lapsed into unconsciousness.[41]

On one of the lower decks, with pieces of wood and metal flying everywhere, M. J. Granfield saw that "some men were crying and fear seemed to be everywhere. I tried to keep my head." Flames began to shoot out of several portholes, and billows of white smoke came up out of the hatches. Many men tried to get through the portholes, but they were too big to fit through the small openings.[42] Finch watched in horror as one young GI, his head out a porthole and his hair on fire, screamed for someone to give him a knife so he could kill himself. He saw another young man whose head, arm, and one shoulder were wedged in a porthole, "so stuck he couldn't move. It made me turn away, sick and crying."[43]

Dr. Boone saw that even on the top deck some planking had buckled, with jagged pieces of it flying into the air. The hatch cover next to his clinic blew off, followed by "repercussions from the boilers" and ammunition explosions from midship. "Pandemonium was immediate," reported the physician, "and the screams of the injured, the crash of falling debris, commingled with shouted orders and calls for help and seeming tremendous vibration of the entire vessel overshadowed everything briefly."[44] The top deck had become littered with all sorts of debris, including soldiers' kits, footlockers, and duffel bags. Many of the wounded were laid out on the poker tables.

Some GIs frantically began climbing up hot pipes to get to the top, seriously burning their hands in the process. Arthur Borows remembers that when the bomb hit, "the stairwells filled with smoke and fire as throngs of screaming men tried to fight their way out." Then Borows noticed the pipes leading to the overhead. "Let's climb up those pipes," he told his friend, Ned. "No," Ned replied, I'm going by the stairways." His friend walked off, and Borows, ignoring the intense heat that burned his hands and shoulders and singed his hair, climbed up a hot pipe, hand over hand, until he reached one of the upper decks.[45]

Rosseau headed for a stairway when the bomb hit but could not locate it in the darkness. Finally he came to an open hatch cover and, on the open rung of the metal ladder going to it, extended his outstretched hand upward and was grasped by someone reaching down. "My foot slipped off the railing, and I was suspended in air, with two or three decks of open hatches, and my possible death below."[46] He was gripped securely, however, and pulled up to the deck by an unknown second lieutenant, who continued to lie flat on the deck and pull other men from the horrifying scene below. Several of the men then formed themselves into human ladders,[47] insisting that the injured go first.

Dr. Edward P. Kelly of Washington, D.C., was on the top deck when the bomb struck, and he immediately ordered some men to lower him by rope through an open hatch to the decks below; he knew his services would be needed there. When he reached the lower decks, he aided the injured as best he could, then tied several GIs to ropes and had them hoisted to the top. Finally, he had to come up himself to restore his own strength; he rested for a while and then tried to go back down, but he was physically restrained from doing so because obviously he was physically exhausted. He survived the *Rohna* and later was awarded the Silver Star for his bravery.[48]

Herman Rice was talking to two sergeants near a ladder when the bomb struck and does not remember the blast itself. "I was standing there, and then there was nothing" as the lights went out and darkness ensued. He began searching for the ladder and, unbelievably, came across one of his buddies from Willard, Ohio, whom he did not know was on the ship. "He was lying on his back with a piece of wood through his leg. I tried to help him—move him—but each time I touched him he screamed." Rice went on and did not see his friend again.[49]

Raymond Epifano was thrown against a bulkhead and knocked out for a short time. When he came to, he spotted one of the few remaining wooden stairways and headed for it. He saw a friend emerge from the galley, bleeding profusely from his head and thoroughly covered with flour.[50] The two climbed the stairway together. Hunter, too, was knocked unconscious when he was thrown into a bulkhead by the blast. When he came to he was "trapped in a literal hell. It was pitch black, the air was full of smoke and steam. I could hear fire under me and the horrifying screams of guys being burned and scalded alive." At that moment Hunter thought of his own mortality and wondered, "What will this do to my poor mother?" Blood ran into his eyes as he blindly began crawling; eventually he found a stairway still intact and managed to get to the top deck.[51]

Chaplain Hewitt felt a "terrific jolt" that buckled his knees and whirled him into the air "as if by the unleashed fury of a cyclone." Like Finch, he started sliding, and he muttered, "We've been hit, and the lights are out. I should have worn my helmet." He thought of his wife, Ruth, and of his mother and father, and of how sad they would be at his loss. Finally Hewitt's slide stopped, and he immediately touched his head and found it stiff and gritty. His fingers were covered with blood, and gradually the realization came to him that he had been wounded. "Strangely enough, this did not seem to be an important discovery to me. It was incredible. I almost wanted to laugh."[52]

He was, the chaplain said, "like a man in a dream." He could see flames from a distance and realized it was a pile of barracks bags. Finally he felt an undamaged bulkhead and inched his way along it until he came to an open hatch. "A dim light was showing from above. It was almost blotted out by smoke and dust. There were steps there, and I felt my way up them into the open air. It was good to be outside. I breathed deeply and thanked God."[53]

Smith had been sergeant of the guard on the night of the 25th, in charge of personnel whose job was to go around the ship at different openings to see that no one was smoking a cigarette or in any other way possibly exposing a light to the enemy. Accordingly, he had relaxed through much of the day on the 26th. When the bomb struck, he realized at once that he was five decks down and that he and his comrades could not go up to the next deck until it had been cleared of escaping GIs. He reckoned his chances of survival to be slim. He went to his barracks bag and took out his wife's picture and his Bible. He could think only of Frances and "how this was going to affect her and that if this was the end how was it going to be." He was beyond fear at this point. He was numb, "but being a Christian, I put it all in God's care."[54]

A man from the 853rd, the battalion that caught the brunt of the attack, later reported that "men were blown from the places they were sitting or standing like leaves in the wind. Mess tables were scattered and thrown about."[55] Hatch covers on decks seven and eight were blown skyward, and many men tumbled down into the open holds. Another remarked, "The whole ship seemed to jump when it [the bomb] hit. The lights went out and smoke was everywhere."[56] A strong smell of cordite instantly permeated the ship.[57] John Walters, from the nearby *Karoa*, and several of his buddies saw the bomb hit the *Rohna*, and they watched with horror and fear as bodies flew up into the air, "their arms and legs like scissors."[58] Also watching from the *Karoa* was Francis Taylor, who was chatting with an English naval doctor when the bomb hit the *Rohna*. He remembers the doctor turning to him and saying, in typical British understatement, "Bit of a blow, that."[59]

But perhaps the doctor on the *Karoa* would not have commented so calmly on the nearby blast had he observed the scene on the *Rohna:* According to one witness interviewed by Carl Molesworth for his book *Air Combat in China*, "as soon as the bomb struck, every sign of order vanished, and it became a fight of survival in which many lives were lost needlessly. As the men recovered from the shock of the explosion sufficiently to move into action, panic spread like wildfire, fanned on by the terrifying screams of the dying and the horrible sight of frantic men clawing their way to the upper decks with clothes on fire and skin hanging loose from their faces and bodies."[60]

One of the only casualties that went unlamented by the men was Neville, Captain Murphy's pet goat—hit by a falling beam, so it was said. Many lascars midship and in the front—where the damage was not as severe—slit their own goats' throats in what was perceived by observers to be some sort of Indian ritual. Then several lascars huddled together in a corner and "went into another world," hoping for deliverance from this catastrophe. Most reports surmised that these lascars died, because they were never seen again.[61]

Many men, now sensing instinctively that the ship would not be saved, worked their way to the open holes on both the port and starboard sides and jumped into the water. A radio operator wrote later: "I was knocked unconscious for about 15 minutes. After recovery, I managed to crawl through a hole where the . . . bomb had entered, and lower myself to the sea." Another soldier at the starboard grasped a lifeboat rope that was being lowered. Just then the rope broke, caused by the weight of many other men already hanging on, bringing the entire lifeboat down on top of those already in the water, killing many of them. The soldier, according to eyewitnesses, was caught between the capsized lifeboat and the *Rohna* but managed to escape. Likely many of these first men off the ship were saved because they could see the *Pioneer* and *Atherstone* in the distance and immediately began swimming toward them.

But the men at the port-side hole recall one heroic sight: Red Cross representative Sparks coming down a rope and, rather than abandoning ship, actually going into her to try and save lives. Brewer later remarked in admiration: "I will never forget his courage."[62]

Although some men jumped out of one of the two holes in the *Rohna,* most calculated that their chances of survival would be better if they could get to one of the upper decks. "When the wood stopped flying," said one survivor, the men were ordered to get to the top as best they could. Peach remembered that everyone seemed to walk up whatever stairways were available, in pairs. He found one of his officers, Major Wagner, and the two walked up a stairway, "hand in hand, like two children going to kindergarten." Peach said, "Had it not been for Wagner I would have given way to the terror that possessed me, and I would have permitted myself to become a nervous wreck, but because he remained cool I overcame some of my fear and I stayed reasonably calm."[63]

Like many other GIs arriving at the top, Peach was awed by what he saw. When he looked at the deck, he was shocked: "The ship was listing, and black smoke was coming from the aft deck." After getting over the initial wonderment, Peach exclaimed, "Oh, my God!" He was quick to explain that his outburst was not intended as a profanity, but "as a prayer. I was sure my end had come." After standing on deck for a few minutes, Peach realized he had someone else's helmet on. "I foolishly ran down four flights of stairs, over fallen hatch-way covers," and exchanged helmets. Using the dim light from a hatch cover, he got back on deck and rejoined Major Wagner.[64]

As soon as some order was restored, the men on the top deck realized their plight and decided that if they were going to survive they would have to jump over the railings. They knew that doing so would be fraught with its own disadvantages and perils.

Chapter 4

Over the Railings

GIs, 26 November: 5:16–5:30 P.M.

In the next quarter hour pandemonium set in, causing deaths and injuries that probably could have been avoided had there been prior exercises in evacuating a stricken ship. Order quickly went by the wayside.

In their efforts to get from the lower decks, desperate men jammed the wooden stairways that were still usable so that nobody could move, further harming those already injured. The first thing Brewer did when he reached topside was look over the *Rohna*'s port side to see the huge, gaping hole and watch clouds of steam rise as the water went into the fiercely burning engine room. Brewer realized at that moment that he would have to abandon the vessel.[1]

Inks confirmed Brewer's estimate of the situation: "I did not know the extent of the damage until I arrived up on the main deck to find our ship listing precariously to starboard and the water already full of men. No one had to tell you to abandon ship as you could feel the ship sinking beneath your feet."[2]

Many from the lower decks seemed surprised that there had been casualties above. They saw GIs writhing in pain on the top deck, while an officer, waving a pistol, furiously ordered them to abandon ship.[3] Nearby, another officer shouted, "No, do NOT abandon ship." Yet another officer held his gun on a young enlisted man and relieved him of his life belt.[4] Lieutenant Colonel Frolich went to the bridge, where Captain Murphy told him to order his men to the boat stations, which he subsequently did "by word of mouth because the ship's signal system was out of order." Another naval officer, however, instructed Frolich not to abandon ship because "we might float yet." The order to abandon ship, it later was pointed out, "is not done the same in all cases." It depends on *how* the ship is sinking. It was optimism and optimism alone, however, that caused some of the officers to believe that the *Rohna* might right herself.[5] British cadet W. L. Butcher noted that it was impossible to give any boat station alarm because of the noise and panic that began to develop. Butcher shouted at the men as they arrived at the top to go to the foredeck and stay there, because he felt it was just possible that the ship would right itself and float. No one could hear him. Butcher reported further that he saw many of the ship's officers throwing secret papers and confidential codes overboard in specially weighted boxes. Watching the officers convinced many of the men for the first time that the ship truly was sinking.[6]

But some of the men still did not believe they would have to leave the ship. "No," said one, even as he looked out over the water and saw "heads bobbing like coconuts," this is not happening. He believed the pumps and engines would start operating again, "and we will be saved." Forrest "Bill" Wheeler, seeing men in the water already drifting away, said to himself, "This can't be that serious—those guys will have to get back on board, wet, cold, and miserable!"[7] Finch was ecstatic to get to the top deck, but his elation subsided when he saw "those brown-clad figures out there in the water." He asked, "why are those damn fools jumping overboard? . . . I never gave it a thought that the ship might be sinking."[8]

Conversely, many men reached the top and in a very orderly fashion took off their shoes and neatly lined them up against a bulkhead, apparently anticipating their jumps overboard.[9] Parker Childress was one of these men. "We all stood in line undressing, taking our shoes off, folding our clothes in military style as if we were going swimming and coming back to claim them."[10] Herald Miles saw two soldiers standing at a railing, calmly devouring a box of stateside chocolate bars before jumping overboard.[11]

Diehl, quickly recovering from his "appendicitis," felt the top deck getting hot. He found a young man from the motor pool with a head wound; taking cloth from his pocket, he bandaged the GI's wound, "put a nice big bow in it and let him go." Diehl was unable to dislodge another soldier, holding on to a pipe and frozen in that position. No amount of persuasion could get him to move. Diehl left his 45-caliber pistol with him and moved on.[12] An officer ordered Mason and some of his buddies to try to break the lock-grip that many soldiers had on the railings, inflate their life belts, and throw them into the water. Mason and his comrades were only partially successful. "Some we could not break their holds on the rails, and I guess they were still there when the ship went down."[13]

Many soldiers stopped what they were doing when they saw an infantryman arrive on the top deck in full field uniform. His helmet was strapped on his head, his shoes highly polished, and he had a knapsack on his back and a rifle on his shoulder. Everyone hooted at him because, as John Canney remembers, "we thought he was a comedian." Their amusement soon turned to horror as the young man headed quickly toward the railing. Before anyone could restrain him, he jumped overboard. "In silence," Canney said, "we stared at the water, but he never reappeared."[14] Another GI jumped from the deck with his jacket full of C rations, sinking immediately into the sea and never resurfacing.

Many of these men—particularly if they jumped from the port, or high, side—had their necks broken on impact with the water and subsequently were lost. Smith looked over the side of the *Rohna* and saw men struggling in the water, shoulder to shoulder, "some already floating tail up," others hurt and unable to swim.[15]

Perhaps fewer of these men would have died had they learned to use their life belts properly. But apparently because of lack of officer initiative and lack of soldier interest, complete instructions never were given. Before they left Oran, the troops had been ordered to wear the life belts at all times, especially when asleep. About four inches wide, they were worn around the waist and inflated by squeezing levers in the belt that would pierce two CO_2 cartridges. If this automatic inflation failed, one could inflate it by mouth using two tubes with screw-type valves on the ends.

The belts had been given to the men after they boarded the ships. "The preservers were issued rather haphazardly," one witness remembered. Crates of life belts were broken open, and the men grabbed them as best they could through the jostling crowds that encircled them. And they were never given any instructions on the proper use of the waist-type life belt. No one ever told them, for example, that they could—and perhaps should under dire circumstances—put it up under their armpits. Many GIs inflated their life belts around their waists and jumped into the water. Some dived into the Mediterranean head first with such force that the life belts popped right off their middles. Others were found later with heads and feet submerged and their middles—with life belts still in place—floating. One officer had attempted to gather men around him to explain how to use the life belts. Many of the men, however, walked away; they had more "important" things to do.[16]

And at the time of the attack, some of the CO_2 cartridges already had been expended. Perhaps to make up for the disappointment of the Thanksgiving dinner or to relieve boredom, a few GIs had begun to play jokes on each other. Some GIs liked to sneak up behind a man, reach around his right side, and squeeze the lever, puncturing the CO_2 cartridge. As the belt inflated, it sounded as though the wearer were having a huge attack of flatulence—much to the delight of those around him. As a result of these pranks, later in the water, many men did not have the strength to orally inflate their life belts, costing some their lives. A few men had the foresight to realize they might be attacked and hid their cartridges in their pockets.

Some physical violence erupted over the CO_2 cartridges. Finch saw "some pretty bloody fights going on as people fought to get their cartridge there at the rail."[17] One man, however—who still had his cartridge—tried to inflate his preserver by mouth. "Someone yelled to him that that was not necessary and all he had to do was squeeze the lever to puncture the CO_2 cylinders. His belt was already partially inflated, so when he discharged the cylinders, the end was blown off his preserver. Since there were no spare belts available, there is little doubt of the fate that awaited that man."[18] An officer on the top deck was in a wild state of panic, "upsetting everybody." A sergeant hit him into semiconsciousness, leaned over him, activated his life belt, and threw him overboard.[19] Whether the officer survived or not is unknown.

Many soldiers found their prayers answered when they reached the top deck, squeezed the lever, and saw their life belts inflate. Conversely, Bill McKee experienced the nightmare the men feared. His belt inflated at first, but as he helped many men go overboard, it was accidentally pierced and thus was of no use to him. Fortunately he was a strong swimmer.[20] Peach did not realize there were two canisters for each life belt. Many hours later, after he had been rescued—and to his astonishment—the second one went off, and he realized he had survived with a half-inflated life belt.[21]

Many survivors of the *Rohna* believed (and still do) that everyone's chances would have been better had they been issued Mae West life preservers (designed to be worn around the chest, vest style) instead of the waist type. (The Indian crew had vests, with small red signaling lights sewn into them.)

Almost every subsequent board of inquiry into the *Rohna* tragedy recommended improvements in life belts worn by American personnel. Most often, the recommendation was for a Mae West-type of life jacket instead of the CO_2 cartridge-type life belt. Or if not a Mae West, then a "Kapok" jacket should be used, because this type would have provided warmth in the water and, more importantly, would have rendered the upper body more buoyant and made it easier to keep one's head afloat. Another suggestion frequently made at boards of inquiry was that every soldier, even before sailing, be put into the water wearing a life belt to get him accustomed to it and to make him confident with it in any subsequent emergencies. "Practice would have made perfect," said one survivor, "and ensured that men did not forget instructions in the event of an emergency."[22]

Also contributing to the grim situation on the *Rohna* was the inadequate number and poor condition of the lifeboats. While the *Rohna* carried two thousand passengers, she was equipped with only twenty-two lifeboats, fourteen of which were stowed near the outside rails with the other eight stowed inboard. Six lifeboats were destroyed in the bomb attack itself; a few others could not be lowered because the steel platings on both sides of the ship had been blown upward and outward in the blast, making it impossible to get lifeboats by them. And as the men quickly discovered, those that were left were largely unusable. Horton saw at once that "they were old, beaten up things"; the bottom of one lifeboat was so rotten that a man's foot went right through it when he stepped on board.[23] Most reports indicate that altogether some six lifeboats were ultimately lowered; of these, only two worked properly.

Third Officer J. M. Buckler, who rescued
T. J. Murphy, captain of the *Rohna*, from
the sea.

British Third Officer Buckler, however, maintains that the lifeboats were in good condition. Most of the boats on the port side
could not be lowered, he said, because of the blast. Boats still were
dropped onto the platings that had been blown outward by the
bomb in the hopes they eventually would float free once the water
hit them. "Immediately prior to the attack," however, all of the lifeboats were "in excellent working order and were thoroughly checked
regularly."[24]

Nevertheless, there were an extraordinary num-
ber of problems with the lifeboats. Some had tangled lines, many

of which had to be cut through with axes and hatchets. Others had rusted cables that would not yield when the davits and blocks were tested. And even if these conditions had not existed, most lifeboats could not have been lowered because of the multiple layers of paint on the tracks and other mechanisms by which they would be lowered into the sea. Thinking he could activate a lifeboat by forcing the rusty hinge on the lowering mechanism to give way, Tech. Sgt. Walter D. Zielinski searched for a large hammer to do the job. Finding none, he tried to do the job with his GI shoes, but "it was a useless attempt."[25] Another man tried to break the same hinge with the butt of his rifle. The butt broke, shattering into pieces. Eventually Zielinski, at least, found another boat and ultimately was rescued.

Quick saw several soldiers—twenty-five or thirty of them—pile into a lifeboat that was still hanging from a cable on both ends. Suddenly, one end of the cable snapped, causing the lifeboat's front end to drop sharply downward. All the men were "dumped on top of one another into the sea." Quick surmised that not only the cables, but the latches, davits, and blocks as well were so rusted that they couldn't be released, "and in their panic, the men did not consider the dangerous situation they were creating."[26]

Richard Ferguson looked toward the ship's stern and saw a lifeboat full of people, but no one knew how to work the mechanisms. The passengers tried frantically to cut the ropes and cables with axes and knives, causing one end to release before the other; the boat then began spinning and swinging, accelerating crazily with each roll of the ship, spilling all except one into the water some thirty feet below.[27] When the lifeboat stopped spinning, the men on deck saw Vernon Kramer still desperately clinging to the boat. At that moment, the boat broke free from the remaining rope (many of the ropes later were found to be rotten) and fell, killing not only many of its previous occupants, but also some who already had jumped off the *Rohna* and were trying to swim away. Kramer disappeared into the turmoil of the men below and the churning sea but managed to survive the ordeal: When the boat hit the water, he was thrown clear "and just swam away."[28]

One of the bitterest aftermaths of the *Rohna* tragedy concerned the actions of the Indian crew. Almost all of the GIs felt the lascars had misled them regarding the use of the lifeboats. Even when boat drills had been conducted, the British officers merely checked to make sure the Americans were wearing their life belts and had a full canteen of drinking water. No instructions were ever given to these soldiers on how to prepare and operate the lifeboats in case of an emergency; apparently this was the lascars's responsibility.

But in fact the lascars apparently proved again the old truth that self-preservation is the most basic instinct. In one incident, a group of Indians lowered one workable boat, only to have it turn over before it reached the water. Canney said the boat jammed on its aft end while the front continued to descend, "spilling out its terrified human cargo." He reported further that "their grotesque movements to stay with the boat was reminiscent of a clip from an old silent movie comedy."[29] An official report from the U.S. Adjutant General's office claimed that the lascars had no thoughts in the emergency for anyone but themselves.[30] Apparently the lascars also panicked on the *Rohna*'s sister ship, the *Karoa*: They tried to lower a lifeboat, even though the *Karoa* was not hit. This action enraged one of the British gun crew. "You bloody bastards!" he shouted, "Get back on this ship, or we'll blow you out of the water!" They hastily complied and disappeared below deck.[31]

Only a few GIs were willing to give the lascars the benefit of the doubt. "Perhaps they were novice sailors", said Finch, "and may have had no training . . . in the handling of lifeboats." On the top deck, he recalled, they "ran around screaming," sometimes "slugging one another" to get the best vantage points.[32] One of the lascars, however, Serang Bhowan Meetha, received special praise from Wells, the *Rohna*'s second officer. "He did outstanding work," said Wells, "in his efforts to get the boats away." Meetha was very composed in the face of the emergency, and although his face was badly burned, he rendered "valuable assistance" throughout the ordeal.[33] Finch's fellow Texan, Hand, also defended the lascars. "Those people were little," he exclaimed, with each weighing about ninety pounds and able to "stand under my arm." They were hired to swab decks and be cook-bearers for the officers—all for about thirty rupees a month. "They were not actually trained for anything else," Hand reports, "I really don't think they should be blamed." He believed the British officers should be held responsible, however, "for apparently giving GIs the false impression that the lascars were 'expert' at handling the boats."[34]

While many of the men on the *Rohna* struggled with the life-boats, others fared no better with the 101 rubber life rafts, which came in various sizes. Some were small enough for men to throw overboard. Many of the larger ones, however, were glued to the angled iron slides by the multiple coats of paint that had been applied while the *Rohna* was tied up in Oran and before. Those not "painted shut," as one GI called it, were released by cutting the ropes that held them in place. Because of their weight, however, once they were cut loose there was no way to keep them from dropping into the sea. Some of the rafts plunged thirty to forty feet, hitting many frantic swimmers and injuring or killing them. Many of the rafts hit the water upside down and could not be righted by exhausted men. Others quickly capsized as hundreds of soldiers fought to get on board.

Making matters worse, there were no usable life-sustaining provisions in the rafts: no drinking water, first-aid kits, C or K rations, or signaling devices. And the oars had been tied in the rafts so tightly and with such thick lines that they could not be readily released. Some men, unable to cut the oars loose, were left to drift wherever the Mediterranean would take them.

But as grim as the situation was on the water, it was on the top deck where greater disorder prevailed, with everyone, it seemed, rushing to the lifeboats, life rafts, and soon even the railings. Many of these soldiers who kept fighting for position lost their lives. Interest-ingly, the ones who held back, smoked a couple of ciga-rettes, and watched the men at the rail cry, fight, and struggle with each other generally survived the ordeal ahead of them.

Finch and his buddies, for example, talked about their chances of being picked up if they did go into the water and kept hoping "for some sort of a miracle to happen to keep us from going in." From their vantage point the sea looked cold and uninviting, and they wanted to wait as long as possible before going over the side. Finally, when they knew it was either sink or swim, they "started for the rail once again" and prepared to hit the water.[35]

GIs, 5:16–5:50 P.M.: Over the Side

Fifteen minutes after the bomb struck, the ship literally was slip-ping out from under the men's feet. Nevertheless, the ship's gunners continued to fire at the remaining German aircraft until the list became so pronounced that their guns were rendered useless. The *Rohna* was going down by the stern and listing heavily on the star-board side, which also was almost completely engulfed in smoke, making it impossible to see any rescue craft that might be nearby. From the port side, however, the view was clear, so most men clam-bered to the port-side railings, which now were about twenty feet from the sea on the stern, thirty-five feet in the middle, and fifty feet on the bow. And, remembering their instructions always to leave on the high side whenever abandoning ship, they jumped. Some of the soldiers, however, fearing such a high jump, went off the starboard side, and of these, many were sucked back through the gaping hole in the *Rohna* and perished.

One exception was Simon Muchnick. He crawled down a rope on the starboard side and dropped into the water about ten feet below. He managed to get away from the ship's suction and grab onto a piece of debris and float away.[36] John Paskowski swam away from the *Rohna*, only to be sucked back into the ship. Several men grabbed him and took him to one of the top decks, where he was told to jump. He couldn't, "or wouldn't," jump, as he recalls, so he told his comrades to throw him over—which they did.[37]

When Mason jumped from the starboard side and hit the water, he tried to swim away, but like many others he was caught in the water rushing into the *Rohna*'s hole. Adding to his problems, he still wore his heavy combat boots. Once he was able to remove them, he swam laboriously toward the ship's stern. Another GI grabbed him and asked for help, "although he seemed to be doing as well as I."[38] The two swam together to the stern, then, because of a "friendly," well-timed wave, began drifting away from it.

But even those men jumping off the port side had to fight a heavy current. Bauer jumped off the bow and began swimming to get away from the ship. The current was so strong that it "swept me past the site where the bomb hit. It was a hole you could drive a Mack truck through.[39] Schoenacker tried to time his jump to hit the crest of a wave, because he thought doing so would carry him far enough away from the ship to keep from being pulled under, but he was unsuccessful. Once in the water (he could not find his "crest"), he floated by the huge hole on the port side and twice was pulled under the ship.[40] Because of the current, Meyer Bronstein "knew enough not to fall off into the incoming wave and be smashed against the side." He waited for a wave's crest to come in and dropped off into its trough. He then floated with the crests and swam through the troughs, "a process I learned from my brief encounters with the breakers at the Jersey shore." By constantly repeating this process, Bronstein "even began to enjoy it and found myself making headway without exhausting myself."[41]

Other men, rather than simply leaping into the sea, used other means to lower themselves. Phythian took off his shoes, zipped up his jacket, said a quick prayer, and went down a rope. His hands started to burn, but he remembered a gym teacher from grade school days who had taught the class that if they went hand over hand while descending a rope they wouldn't burn their hands.[42] Later, in a report on the *Rohna*, Bronstein suggested that all seagoing soldiers be equipped with leather gloves to prevent rope burns in emergency situations.[43]

After telling his men that everyone was on their own, Sgt. Harry Cullings climbed down a cargo net and jumped the rest of the way into the water. When he hit the Mediterranean, he reached for his life belt to inflate it, but found he had lost it going overboard. He swam vigorously away from the *Rohna* to escape its suction and quickly tired. Even worse, he did not know how to float. So he thought, "What is the use of struggling? This is it." He took off his helmet and slid under the water, believing that it would take only two or three minutes for him to drown and that he would not suffer terribly. But then he thought, "This is no way to go. I am going back up and struggle to the end." He labored to the surface and quickly spotted a raft with a line floating from it. "The Lord must be with me," he thought, as he swam toward the line, caught it, and was pulled on board the raft.[44]

Lieutenant Brewer wrapped his legs around a rope and held on desperately as he descended toward the water. It was slow going "because there were men one next to another all the way to the water." At one point, someone just above him on the line stood on his hands, apparently to rest. It turned out to be a friend; Brewer yelled at him to move. Brewer then continued down, and about twenty feet above the water his rope broke, "dumping several men below into the water." Brewer and his friend were able to grab an adjacent rope and continue their descent. "It wasn't long until I reached the water and began to float outward to sea."[45] Brewer did not report on the fate of his friend.

Fievet's drop into the sea was impeded by his friend, John Fallon, who was below him and could not break his grip on the *Rohna.*

Fievet kicked away from the ship's hull to keep from hitting Fallon and went off into the sea. (It was not until 1993 that Fievet learned Fallon's body had been recovered from the sea sometime in December 1943.)[46] Fievet's watch stopped exactly at 5:50 P.M. as he hit the water. (Decades after the war, Fievet still has the watch, frozen in time at exactly ten minutes before six.)[47] Remarkably, one of the first persons he met in the water was his friend and fellow Alabaman, Childress. He looked at the overweight Childress and called to him, "Where you going, Blubber?"[48] Unfortunately, the two friends soon were separated as they drifted out into the sea.

Brewer and Fievet were two of the fortunate ones. Others who stayed on the deck until the last moment reported later that they saw many men hanging head down—sometimes their heads actually were submerged—with their legs and arms hopelessly entangled in ropes, lines, rope nets, and rope ladders.

One Red Cross worker was able to work loose a rope net on which several men could descend, but halfway down it became congested with literally hundreds of men hanging on. Some were able to grab adjacent ropes; others fell straight into the sea and never were seen again. Captain Murphy could not remember how he got away from the ship. "I remember being showered with shellcases . . . and being in the water almost immediately, hurt in many places."[49]

While many of these men were on the lines and nets leading down into the sea, a German plane reappeared (possibly a Junkers 88) on a strafing mission. A soldier on a line next to Finch was hit in the head, splattering blood all over. Later, after the airplane left and as the men drifted, several noted with dismay that the strafer had forced rescue ships to change their courses or turn around altogether to escape the gunfire. This would make it, they knew, more difficult for the ships to rescue them—if they were rescued at all.

Chapter **5**

The End of the *Rohna*

Germans, 26 November: 5:30–9:30 P.M.

While the men of the *Rohna* struggled in the water, Dochtermann and his crew were winging their way home to Bordeaux in the company of several of their surviving compatriots. Flying in a west-northwest direction, Dochtermann saw the Spanish island of Gaudilio Franco far below him and knew he was approaching Spain's three-mile zone; accordingly, he and the other pilots steered their craft along the coast in "respectful observance" of that country's neutrality in World War II.[1]

Up ahead they could see the lights of Barcelona and were awed at their beauty. The greatest inspiration, though, was Radio Andorra. Many German soldiers were familiar with this

station in Andorra, nestled in the Pyrenees mountains between
Spain and France about 3,000 meters up (some 10,500 feet) and
some 100 kilometers (about 62.5 miles) north of Barcelona; they
liked the "hot" music, usually a mixture of jazz and swing, that was
constantly beamed out over its airways. Moreover, German pilots
returning from Med-iterranean raids used Radio Andorra as a navigation aid. It helped them to locate their own radio frequencies
coming out of Bordeaux and other French cities. On this night,
though, Dochtermann and his crew were not as concerned with
radio direction as with the beautiful, seductive, melodic voice of the
French-speaking young lady who introduced the music. Radio man
"Rambo" kept the music coming into the earphones of the entire
crew. "For a short while," Dochtermann remembers, there was a
"breath of tranquility, youth, and happiness" among his crew.[2]

The reverie was short-lived, however. Rambo received word from
the Bordeaux/Merignac area that the weather there was terrible.
Deep hanging clouds, mist, rain, and fog shrouded the region.
Cognac, 120 kilometers north of Bordeaux, was their recommended
alternate destination. The weather there, while not perfect, was better than in Bordeaux. Dochtermann and most of the other Heinkel
177 pilots were skilled at landing in bad weather; in fact, in their
training days, many had used onboard instruments automatically
(blind flying) to land their aircraft. Since Cognac was so near, however, and the pilots could make fairly clear landings, the German
officials felt it was pointless to have them land with instruments in
very bad weather at Bordeaux.[3]

The German squadron flew in from the south over Cognac at
about three hundred meters (roughly nine hundred feet). All the
lights were burning at the runway, though it was still misty. There
were two hangars on either side of the runway, which became the
point of reference for the pilots. Schmidt told Dochtermann he
thought their plane could land without problems. Dochtermann
was aware, however, that in such misty weather vertical vision (the

sight down to the runway) might be good, but the horizontal vision, when one is just a few feet above the runway, is usually wretched, with at least a temporary loss of the line of sight, making it difficult to adjust to wind and other variable factors. As if to prove his point, the plane in front of Dochtermann "thundered" onto the runway at high speed and engine velocity and slipped off onto soft ground behind a hangar, where it broke apart. Dochtermann learned later that four men in the cockpit lost their lives, while those in the fuselage survived.[4]

Dochtermann landed his plane safely at 9:30 P.M. He had been in the air for seven hours and thirty-five minutes. He and his crew were ushered into a situation office and ordered immediately to write a report about their day's activities. It was difficult for Dochtermann (and the recording secretary) to put down on paper his direct hit on a troop transport, because he feared some of his superiors would deem his report "unbelievable." Dochtermann, of course, had not personally witnessed the actual strike, because he had been busy maneuvering the plane. A colleague, Oberweldwebel (similar to a first lieutenant in the U.S. Army Air Forces) H. Matschke, however, reported that he had lingered in the convoy's vicinity after the attack and viewed the stricken ship, watching it sink into the Mediterranean.[5]

Dochtermann also learned the fate of some of his colleagues. His comrade, Richard Wiesner, an experienced aviator and veteran of numerous raids over the Atlantic, Mediterranean, and Adriatic, took many hits from the combined fire of the ships in the convoy. His hydraulic equipment had been knocked out, forcing him to operate, with great difficulty, most of the rudders (one would not work at all), as well as his landing gear, by hand. Some of the automatic landing equipment, such as landing flaps, was lost as well, and the plane's engines began to overheat. It took great strength and perseverance for Wiesner to fly his aircraft over the Mediterranean and bring it in for a nighttime landing at Montpelier. But he came in just short of the runway, landing in the darkness in a lagoon off the airport. Wiesner's bombardier, sitting beside him in the cockpit, drowned. Wiesner and the rest of the crew survived.[6]

While Wiesner was trying to land in Montpelier, Dochtermann busily completed the necessary forms and reports concerning the attack on KMF-26, then began to look for some food and drink. In the mess hall all the officers, whether they had flown over the Mediterranean that day or not, were far less interested in who won the base casino's jackpots than in hearing about the attack on an Allied convoy and the sinking of a troopship. "Sleep," Dochtermann recollects, "was unthinkable." At long last, however, the conversations, celebrations, and dining broke up, and everyone made for their beds. Dochtermann knew from talking with a meteorologist friend that tomorrow would be a slightly overcast day, but it would be good enough for him to fly back to Bordeaux/Merignac. He and his mates were anxious to do so, because they knew they would be greeted as heroes by their commanders and friends and that there would be many celebrations.[7]

When he got into bed, however, he could not sleep; in fact, he lay awake for the remainder of the night. His adrenaline level was still high, and he could not take his mind off the attack that had taken place earlier. He had not come away from the assault on KMF-26 "unaffected."

GIs, 26 November, 5:50–6:30 P.M.: In the Mediterranean

When a man jumped off the *Rohna*, his chances of hitting an empty spot in the sea were practically nil. In all likelihood he crashed into another man or a boat; or, the instant he hit the water, someone from above fell on top of him, injuring or killing both in the process.

And even if he fell clear of these obstacles, he still had to contend with the heavy scum of oil that now lay over the water as it escaped from the fiercely burning *Rohna*. (Some reports noted that the high columns of water landing on the ships after near misses contained "small drops of what appeared to be oil,"[8] giving rise to the belief that the guided bomb was filled with incendiary oil—a supposition that was never confirmed).

Don Zirkle, along with all of his other comrades, was so heavily coated with the oil that he felt as though he had "been dipped in chocolate." Moreover, the oil in many places was on fire, and he could feel his scalp being seriously singed. As he tried to swim away, a lifeboat came crashing down, hitting his left knee and hip, causing him to sink once again into the Mediterranean. Even before he had left the *Rohna*'s deck, Zirkle felt a severe stinging in his buttocks and realized he had been hit by flying debris after the bomb struck; now that his knee and hip were injured, it was all he could do to swim away from the stricken vessel.[9]

Brewer floated in a sea of oil and debris. "Some of those men," he said, "at the end of their endurance, were grabbing at others in a desperate attempt to stay afloat." His most immediate problem, Brewer said, was to cope with waves full of oil, giving him "mouthfuls of terrible stuff." It was not, however, "difficult to throw it up!"[10] Miles swam vigorously to get away from what he termed a "burning hell," but even then he did not realize that his chances of being rescued were slim.[11]

Red Cross assistant field director Aaron Weinstein's teeth chattered so much in the water that his entire body began to shake, and he felt his life belt slipping away from him. He described his feelings in Tom Suchan's article, "Voyage of Death": "In that awful moment I felt I had to live. I had to see my wife who was having our first child. I had to see that child. I called 'Ruth, Ruth,' over and over again." And then an oar floated over to him and he held on with every ounce of strength he had. Soon, however, he felt the oar slipping from his grasp, and he let go, once again alone in the water. "I felt slimy all over. . . . Only later I realized that I had been floating in oil."[12]

The oil penetrated the men's skin to such an extent that it took some several weeks after their rescue to get rid of it altogether. The men also frequently were burned to incapacity by the ignited oil, or it filled their eyes, blinding them. Phythian recalls seeing GIs who "were burned by the burning oil real *bad*."[13] When Aaron Weber was rescued after about eight hours in the water, the crew of the *Holcombe* wiped him down in an effort to remove the oil. "It took three months before all the oil had been eliminated from my scalp."[14] The oil's only redeeming factor was that it penetrated the skin to such an extent that, especially for those who were in the sea for a long time, it gave some protection against the ever-increasing coldness of the water.[15]

But the men were to have no other relief. The German planes returned again on a strafing run. It was easy for the strafers to see their way clearly in the early night, not having to grope in darkness to find their victims. The huge blaze that came from the burning ship could be seen for miles around. Most of the air escorts had left the area at nightfall, apparently believing that the surface vessels could take care of any further contingencies.

About thirty feet away from where Roy Jacobsen was swimming, he saw some fifteen men desperately hanging on to an overturned lifeboat. Suddenly a German plane swooped down and began to strafe them. "I saw the tracer bullets come down from overhead and I heard them [the GIs] scream in terror as they were blown apart." The plane came in so low that Jacobsen could see—or so he thought—the pilot sitting in the cockpit, with, so it seemed to Jacobsen, a grinning snarl on his face.[16] Raymond Boylan confirmed Jacobsen's observations: "[T]he Germans kept coming back repeatedly, flying low and strafing the water. It was a weird feeling floating in the Mediterranean . . . with no idea whether you were going to live or die."[17] Quick looked up at the strafer and saw what looked like blowtorches burning on the leading edges of the plane's wings.[18]

The lascars, wearing Mae West life preservers when they went into the water, began to turn on the small red lights that came with the equipment, giving the German strafers an added advantage. The GIs repeatedly told the lascars not to use these lights,[19] but, largely out of sheer terror, the lascars continued to shine them. Finally, it was necessary for some soldiers to swim over to the lascars and remove the red lights by force.

One of the worst aspects of the strafing was that it caused some of the rescue ships in the area to pull back. Cunigan, on board the *Pioneer,* said his ship backed up and then suddenly thrust forward to avoid being strafed. There was a life raft directly behind the *Pioneer* at that point, and the ship's screws violently sucked it under, with about eight men on board. "It couldn't be helped," he recalled sadly. "There was no sure way to guide the *Pioneer,*" or any other rescue ships for that matter, out of harm's way, resulting in even more lost lives.[20]

Another reason the rescue ships were forced to back off was that sometimes, in their eagerness to save the men, they came too close to one another, risking crushing some of the very men they were trying to rescue. As a result, they had to leave the immediate area, sometimes stranding the men in the middle of a rescue. The *Pioneer,* for example, once had to move to keep from being run down. "She pulled out," said one witness, "and left men just about to board."[21]

Seeing the rescue ships wheeling off gave Hunter "an awful feeling of abandonment."[22] After the strafings on the rope nets and in the water, activity seemed to stop for several minutes. Then Peach saw another low-flying German plane approaching. He called to one of his buddies, "Is he strafing us again?" He didn't know that this time the pilot was not on a strafing mission: He apparently was taking photographs to record the damage done to KMF-26 in general and the *Rohna* in particular.[23] Loper also remembers a Dornier 217 flying slowly at what he estimated to be an altitude of forty-five feet, coming up on the sinking *Rohna's* starboard side. "I could see the pilot, the copilot, and a third man standing in a crouched manner looking through the aircraft windshield."[24]

The Germans did not have much to fear from the rapidly departing convoy. In fact, the other ships (with the exception of those that had been designated rescue vessels), deeming it essential that the remainder of the convoy reach safety, pushed full speed ahead after the bomb hit the *Rohna*. As the last of the convoy passed the men in the water, Breedlove saw an American ship slow down, and someone with a loudspeaker called out to them: "I'm sorry soldiers, but we have been ordered not to stop and pick up survivors. We wish you all good luck!"[25]

As the *Banfora* steamed away from the men, she had to turn sharply into an "evasive arc" to avoid running over some of the survivors.[26] One of its passengers, Jasper L. Spain, did not have much appetite for food after seeing so many of his comrades out in the water and knowing he could not help any of them. The British officers decided to pass out ample quantities of grog (a mixture of rum and water), perhaps as a way of dealing with their own tensions. Some of the officers became quite drunk; Spain, however, recalled that "the last thing on my mind was getting drunk. I wanted to be in top physical condition in the event I had to swim at any time in the near future."[27] Though there were no more attacks that night, the Allies knew that in all likelihood the Germans (especially German submarines) were still in the area.

By 6:15 P.M. almost all the troops and crew were off the *Rohna*. Captain Murphy, however, along with the second and third officers, remained on board, trying to dislodge the remaining life rafts and boats. The ship's medical officer, Dr. Boone, also stayed on board, as well as several American soldiers too frightened to go over the side. Phythian saw the *Rohna* turn over on her side with men still on board.[28] He never found out whether they got away.

Peach looked back at the *Rohna* and was horrified at the sight of the gaping hole in her. "It extended from the main deck down and

wide enough, it seemed, for a Liberty ship to pass through it."
Someone swimming close to Peach cried out to him, "Better get
away from there; if she goes, she'll take you with her."[29]

Clancy floated alone, held up by his life belt. In the distance he
saw the outline of the *Rohna* burning brightly, lighting up the
nighttime sky, "looking like a big bonfire used to celebrate football
homecoming just a few years before in high school. No celebration
this! I knew I was witnessing the death of HMT *Rohna*."[30]

Finch saw the *Rohna* "completely engulfed in flames, which presented a most memorable spectacle." Showers of sparks and continuing explosions on the ship reminded Finch and others of Indepen-
dence Day celebrations. "Had it not been such a sober occasion,"
Finch said, "the scene would have been most beautiful." Watching
it, the mood that came over Finch was one of gratitude. "How glad
I was that I had not been trapped below deck as so many others had
been. At least by now their suffering was over, I thought."[31] Out in
the water, Gibson looked at the *Rohna,* and, surprisingly, saw an
unlaunched lifeboat not yet touched by the inferno that now practically engulfed the ship. "It stood out against her skeletal aft, silhouetted against the red light of the fire."[32]

As the *Rohna* descended, everyone in the water still in her
vicinity had to use all their strength to get away from the ship's
suction. "No matter how hard I struggled," Finch recalled, "I just
could not get away from that ship." The *Rohna* would roll and
push Finch away, then roll back and suck him in against her side.
"It seemed like an eternity until a huge wave lifted me up and
away from the *Rohna*. I was elated by what I thought was a good
stroke of luck."[33]

Mason saw the *Rohna* finally give the appearance of recovering
from her list. The bow rose sharply, and there was a new shudder-
ing, as if she were in her death throes, and she slipped, stern first,
into the water. Dr. Boone remembers that "the flaming bulk finally
started to roll," and "with great gouts of steam and flame it disap-

peared."[34] Breedlove reported that "I don't imagine any survivor will ever forget watching as the *Rohna*'s rear section, or stern, slid under the water," with "the nose [bow] sticking straight up in the air." Then the bow sank slowly out of sight.[35] Many years afterward, Jacobsen can still "see the *Rohna* on her way to sleep in the deep."[36]

William Caskey's memory of the actual sinking is hazy, but he swears he saw Captain Murphy standing on the bridge, and "I thought I saw a German Shepherd dog standing alongside of him."[37] This was entirely possible, since there were many animals on board. Caskey recalls further that the ship "seemed to go down," then "came back up, still burning." Finally, he saw her go down for the last time.

The *Rohna* sank at approximately 6:30 P.M., close to one hour from the time the guided bomb had plowed into her port side. (For years the rumor floated around that the *Rohna* was salvaged in 1948. There is no hard evidence, however, that such an operation was ever carried out. It is more likely that the ship broke apart on her way to the bottom of the Mediterranean and that her pieces are still there. Nor have any of the confidential code books ever been recovered.)

With the night's approach came the possibility that the burning *Rohna* could serve as a beacon for additional German submarine and air attacks on the rapidly departing convoy. According to numerous eyewitnesses, one of the escort destroyers (possibly the *Atherstone*) returned to the *Rohna* and fired a few shots into her to help her sink, a militarily logical action, since the welfare of the entire convoy was uppermost in the commanders' minds.[38]

Soon after the *Rohna* went down, full darkness fell. Neither the moon nor the stars were fully visible. The only glimmer of hope these men now had was the searchlights they could see from time to time at various points in the distance, giving them the small comfort of knowing that rescue ships were in the vicinity. Even so, these ships were prohibited from keeping their searchlights on for any length of time, lest they attract a new wave of German planes. And these searchlights covered only an infinitesimal area at a time when the current was going out, sweeping men farther and farther out to sea. For most of the men, their biggest ordeals were just beginning.

Some, of course, had been rescued within minutes of the strike. Fortunately for them, no German strafers had arrived at that point. And the *Pioneer* was in the area, as were the British corvette *Holcombe,* tug *Mindful,* freighter *Clan Campbell,* and destroyer *Atherstone*—all designated rescue vessels by Commander Wakeman-Colville at the time the *Rohna* was hit. In addition, a small French tugboat came in from the shores of Algeria. It apparently had been sent by the French naval authorities to tow the *Rohna* back into port in the belief that she could be salvaged. When the tug arrived, however, the crew realized they could not tow the *Rohna* and instead began to pick up survivors.

For those men who had not jumped immediately after the blast, the situation was worse. In the few minutes it took them to jump, oil slicks had formed and the German strafers had arrived. These men ended up in the water the longest and had the highest casualty rates. Ironically, those who remained on board until the *Rohna* was almost submerged faced better odds of surviving than the GIs who had been willing to abandon ship immediately. The strafers had left the area by then, and most oil slicks had dissipated. Thus, those first off and last off were the ones who, for the most part, lived through this horrible ordeal.

The shortest stay in the water was approximately fifteen minutes; the longest, around eleven and a half hours. Throughout the long night men struggled in the water, and personnel on the six rescue vessels became obsessed with rescuing them. None wanted to leave the area until every survivor was safely in their hands.

Chapter 6

"Only" Twenty Miles from Land

GIs, 26 November: 6:31–8:00 P.M.

Among the men who made it, there were lifeboat, life raft, plank, and pole survivors.

After managing to escape the suction caused by the *Rohna* as she sank, Hunter spotted a life raft, half afloat. Wearily he swam toward it and found two of his friends already hanging on. They all managed to get into the life raft and vigorously bail it out with their helmets and shoes. (The heavy steel helmets in most instances proved a hindrance to being rescued because of their weight; it was suggested later that only their liners be retained, since they were just as effective, if not more so, as the helmets themselves in bailing water). Very soon other men, "about six deep," attached themselves to the

85

boat. Hunter noted that "some of these men were horribly burned and the water was full of bodies and drowning men. I can hear those terrible cries to this day."[1] Thomas Hollimon reached a raft with two Indian crew members in it. Together the three picked up men around them until finally there was no room for more either in the raft or on the line trailing from it. The men then held on to each other, forming a large body of humanity floating in the Mediterranean.[2]

Drifting, Bronstein came upon a half-submerged lifeboat full of men. He called out to them to start bailing, but they could not find any bailing equipment. (Later, to their consternation, many men learned that each lifeboat was equipped with lockers under the seats that contained bailing facilities.) Bronstein then tried to bail the water out of the boat with his arms—a useless action without the help of the others. "What did not occur to me until many hardships later," Bronstein recalled, "was that the bulk of the men were too shocked to take action."[3]

Theodore Kroog saw a large circle of men holding hands and saying Hail Marys. One of Kroog's shipmates spotted him and called to him to join the group. He tried, but waves washed the men out of his sight. Knowing he couldn't survive without some kind of support, he managed to find another group hanging on to part of a lifeboat and latched on to it. The motion of the sea against the lifeboat loosened the caps on Kroog's life preserver, causing it to deflate. He tried to blow it up without success. Fortunately for Kroog, a life belt floated by, and he grabbed it. But at that point what remained of the lifeboat began to sink, catching Kroog's pants in the process. He managed to take them off and was left only in his underwear, hoping and praying that he would be rescued.[4] His good fortune in finding a lost comrade's life preserver kept him afloat, but the fate of the others in the lifeboat remains unknown.

Kroog then spotted a man holding on to a large drum and joined him. The soldier, probably from the Army Air Forces, since, Kroog noted, he was wearing a leather jacket, yelled at Kroog to let go, claiming there was not enough room for both of them. After a time, however, the airman stopped protesting, realizing that with Kroog holding on to his jacket, it became easier for the two of them to steady the drum. "I don't know how long we were in the water," Kroog remembered, "but it seemed an eternity."[5]

Not long after Quick jumped from the ship, he saw the first of the many dead he would encounter that night. "He was blond and his face was in the water and I could see the waves swirling through his hair." Quick realized then that even though he had survived the guided bomb's destruction, getting out of this sea alive would be his biggest challenge. He found a life raft with twenty or so men in it, with just as many on the lines extending from it. One soldier was so exhausted that his head kept dropping into the water. Quick supported him until his own strength ran out; then he had to let the soldier go.[6]

Loper considered himself a strong swimmer, but with his injured leg he could do little. Utterly exhausted, he found a lifeboat and was pulled in by a "very skinny" second lieutenant. Loper leaned on another GI as blood oozed out of his mouth onto the soldier's naked back, while that young man "squalled like a small child."[7]

Swimming alone, Peach would see a wall of water all around him one minute, and in the next he would be on top of a wave "looking down at people and things around me." He kept recalling what one of his friends had told him shortly before Peach jumped: "Don't worry, pal, we're only about twenty miles from land." Peach later mused: "Yeah, but he did not say east, west, north, south, or straight down!"[8]

Peach came upon several men holding on to a plank; he joined them when they invited him. "The group of men grew and grew until they were hanging on to one another." Peach saw a member of his company drift by, a "normally cocky but likeable guy," his face now "filled with terror." Peach hauled him on to the plank and made room for him in the group.

"We all began feeling jolly," Peach said, "laughing and talking." Then they began singing "Roll Out The Barrel" as well as touching renditions of "The Star Spangled Banner."[9] But at this point Peach decided it was too crowded on the plank, so he swam away. A bit later, as he swam toward a rescue vessel, he spotted a buddy moving away from it. "You're swimming away from the rescue ship!" Peach called out to him. The young man apparently had given up all hope: "We'll never be saved, Peach!" He was never seen again. Peach then came upon a large Army Air Forces man with close-cropped hair, floating face down. "I lifted his head from the water and his lower jaw sagged." Peach put his arm over the man's shoulder and tried to swim with him toward the rescue ship, but this extra burden weighed him down, and he watched as the vessel moved farther and farther away. "At last I released him and he drifted away. I prayed 'God have mercy on my soul if that man isn't dead!'"[10]

Every time Jacobsen spotted a rescue ship's searchlight, a large wave would crash upon him, making it impossible for rescuers to see him. Ultimately, he "fought the sea" so much and for so long that his legs cramped, causing the muscles to knot up. "Many thoughts went through my mind and I realized I couldn't go on much longer." He finally reached a small group of men on a raft. "I threw myself across the raft, exhausted; I could go no further." The men on the raft were singing, and suddenly someone shouted: "Here comes a ship!" Jacobsen got up on one knee, shouting and waving to attract the rescuers' attention. But suddenly he slipped into unconsciousness and did not come to until he was on board a rescue vessel. To this day he does not know how he was put on board; he simply is thankful that he was.[11]

Dr. Boone joined two others floating on a plank. "[W]e sat, back to back, a clumsy triangle locking arms so that the waves would not wash us away." One of his newfound comrades was Catholic, the other Jewish. "For years I could recall and repeat the prayers of those two: one telling his beads, and the other his Yiddish." Boone had brought along his otoscope. Periodically he held it over his head in the hopes that a rescue ship would spot it. The instrument was, however, quickly short-circuited by the surrounding seawater.[12] Muchnik also found a plank, and he and a dozen other men held on to it "for dear life" for the next five hours, while the rough sea "tossed us as high as twenty feet." Muchnik was twenty-five years old at the time and in the "best physical condition of his life." Otherwise, he believes, "I wouldn't have made it."[13]

Jake Shimp was pushed out by the Mediterranean's northward current and was alone for a "long, long" time. He heard someone else struggling in the water and screaming for help. The two swam toward each other and, in the process, Shimp found a pole about twenty feet long. Shimp and his comrade held on with all the strength they could muster. "I knew I couldn't last much longer," he said, "but I wasn't scared." Suddenly a light flashed over Shimp and his comrade; but the men on board the rescue ship did not see them. "My hopes disappeared. How I felt can't be put into words. I don't think the dictionary has the words to explain it." Later they came across an Indian crew member who yelled that he could not swim and was just about to go under. The lascar held on to Shimp's hand until, out of sheer exhaustion, he let go, and was lost.[14]

Dr. Jackson soon discovered that swimming would only exhaust him, so he turned over on his back and floated. He came to a rescue ship, whose deck looked "to be a mile high." A sailor threw a rope down to him, but Jackson lost sight of it in the darkness. The waves then washed him away from the ship. Soon he heard a large group of men in the water, and when he was close enough, he saw that they were hanging on to some floating life belts. Next to them was a life raft with lines extending over its sides. Jackson found a line and held on. He later said, "I don't believe that a bulldozer could have pulled me off" that rope. The water became increasingly cold, and the men would "almost freeze" when a wave passed over them, then choke when whitecaps hit them in their faces. "We just floated like a piece of wood in the water."[15]

Tom Merker could not swim, but one of his close friends on board the *Rohna* held an American Red Cross swimming license. This friend waited for Merker in the water after he abandoned ship, then pulled him into a lifeboat that contained several other men. When their lifeboat reached a rescue ship, a GI stood up and jumped toward the rescue ladder. The force of his jump pushed the lifeboat away from the ship, which began to steam away, possibly because the rescue crew did not see them. Merker and a few fellow survivors were once again adrift. They spent the next several hours dragging other GIs into their lifeboat.

Merker and his companions decided that, to protect against capsizing, four men should each lean on the four corners of the lifeboat. The other occupants would interlock their hands on the ropes around the circumference of the lifeboat. No one was permitted to stand up anywhere in the lifeboat, although some did anyway, praying to God, crossing themselves, and crying. "It was a sight that I will never ever forget."[16]

Gibson left the ship with two buddies, Donald Keefe and Marion Farrell, both lieutenants. Against Gibson's advice, Farrell jumped into a lifeboat half filled with water and "chocked full of men," with others frantically trying to get on board. "I was sure the boat would capsize"—and it did. Farrell went under, and Gibson never saw him again; Gibson and Keefe swam out into a "clear area" where a frantic soldier grabbed Gibson around the neck. Gibson "talked him off," assuring the man that his life preserver was working "all right."[17]

William Wasp ultimately was saved in large part because of one of his mates, Pvt. 1/C James Pope. When Wasp reached the *Rohna*'s top deck after the guided bomb struck, he found that he had lost his life belt, probably due to the bomb's concussion. He jumped anyway, then called to those around him in the water that he could not swim. Pope dived in, caught Wasp, and told him "to hang onto my fatigues, and kick like hell." Pope, pulling Wasp along with him, swam to a lifeboat. When the lifeboat became too crowded and capsized, Pope again grasped Wasp and swam away with him. For his heroic work in saving Wasp, Pope later was commended for gallantry, winning the Bronze Star.[18] "I didn't think anything about being any kind of hero," he said later. I was just doing what I could to survive and help others survive."[19]

Clancy, who does not remember how he got off the sinking *Rohna*, woke up to find himself floating in the water. He felt a slight rubbing sensation across the front of his shirt and, reaching up to pull it away, found that he was holding a handful of skin. "I then noticed an eerie glow [possibly from being in the water so long] on the backs of both my hands. I knew, almost immediately that, even though I was not feeling any pain, I must have been severely burned on my face and hands."[20]

Clancy drifted for some time and then heard voices in the dark. He swam toward them and found about a dozen men holding on to the side of a lifeboat. "I must have looked like hell," he said, "for they immediately helped me get on the raft." These men managed to stay in and hold on to the sides of the raft until "ten or fifteen" foot waves came through, knocking them off, causing some to sink into the sea and others frantically to get back to the boat. "That happened repeatedly throughout the long, cold night."[21]

The body of a lascar floated by Clancy's boat, a battery-powered light clipped to his life jacket. Taking the light, Clancy pinned it to his own shirt, stuffing the battery down his shirt front. "I then became a beacon to guide the rescue ships we all hoped were coming."[22] Other GIs remained reluctant throughout the night to use their lights. "While we realized the light would help rescue ships to locate us," Quick recalled, "we feared it might also help German aircraft do the same."[23]

Edward Ashley does not remember the circumstances surrounding his rescue. "I linked up with a group of twelve to fourteen men hanging on to some lumber." By midnight, said Ashley, "most of their heads were under water." Finally, he and the remaining men in his group spotted a searchlight, "and that is the last thing I remember." He woke up the next morning in an officer's bed, on board a British ship. He had been picked up at 12:30 A.M., too far "out of it" to ask anyone how his rescuers had known he was alive.[24]

After swimming around for a time, Buckler found a life raft with three Americans on board. Several minutes later, he heard a familiar voice crying out in the watery darkness: It was Captain Murphy. Buckler handed a flashlight to a GI and told him to flash it occasionally as a guide. Then Buckler dived back into the water and swam some fifty yards, found the captain, and brought him to the life raft." By this time he [the Captain] was nearly unconscious."[25]

Some men were fortunate to find something—a lifeboat or raft, plank, or even a piece of rope—to hold on to as they drifted. Others, however, found no such support. Breedlove, for example, unable to find an object to grasp on to, knew he was near enough to land to try and swim for it. The tide, however, was going out, and he quickly realized that putting his back to the waves and riding them as best he could was the right thing to do. "The tide sweeping me out to sea had its advantages." He and thirty of his comrades formed a circle and held hands so they could more easily be seen when or if help came. But eventually "the rough, cold sea began to take its toll." Some men silently slipped under the water; others fought it until they were exhausted, then simply disappeared. Breedlove especially remembers one buck sergeant from Texas who tried to keep his comrades' spirits up by singing, laughing, telling jokes—anything to keep the men going. Finally, though, the young Texan exclaimed, "I'm completely give out and can't go on any longer." He then dropped out of sight. A young Jew "went berserk" and started screaming in Yiddish for his mother. He unbuckled his life belt and went under.[26]

After some time Breedlove noticed that sections of his own life belt were losing air, and he had to keep reinflating it. By then, however, there were several bodies floating around him, so, reasoning that their life belts were not helping them, he took two and used them for the remainder of the night. He and the others in his group could see the lights of rescue ships from the convoy in the distance, "but we couldn't get their attention." When the cold water caused their body temperatures to drop, they began vigorously to move their arms and legs to get the circulation going. But "that tired us more," Breedlove recollects, "so we had to stop it."[27]

Lieutenant Brewer stayed away from groups as much as possible, believing that "solitary swimming" would serve him better. He sustained himself by limning on his brain the image of his wife, Henrietta, who he knew was waiting for him back in Stockton, California. "I remember looking up at the stars and seeing my wife's face. I really imagined her telling me I would make it if I just kept fighting." (After the war he learned that on the date of the sinking, 26 November, his wife actually had dreamed about a ship being sunk and saw him spending the night in the water.) Brewer came to a large, floating mass of people, drifting together and calling for help in unison. Many of these men were wild with panic, having never seen an ocean before or, for that matter, any large body of water. "Many were being drowned right there as they tried to climb up upon each other," Brewer remembered. He left this group, but stayed nearby so he would be more noticeable to any rescue ship that might come through.[28]

He soon became sleepy and began to feel warm all over, a situation that added to his worries, because he feared he was losing consciousness. He kicked his legs violently and yelled as loudly as he could, moving back toward the mass of men. "Their panic had subsided," he found; or else exhaustion had overwhelmed them. Still in unison, the group—now quietly—called for help, and then one man began reciting the Lord's Prayer, which was repeated by everyone else. Then someone exclaimed that he could see a search-light coming in their direction. "I imagined my wife smiling at me," Brewer recalled later.[29]

Ernest Goen, swimming alone, drifted in the darkness toward what he perceived to be Italy, and thought, "I sure don't want to get captured!" He paddled to a group of eighty to a hundred men and hung on. "Once in a while what I thought were sharks bumped into my legs, but they turned out to be porpoises." Like his mates, Goen exercised his legs against the cold and swallowed quantities of salt water. "And I'd hear people cry 'goodbye mother' and 'goodbye sweetheart.'"[30]

As he drifted, Ferguson found a lifeboat, but it was full of water and men, with additional GIs grasping its rims; still, he managed to grab hold of it and hang on. A lascar could not find room at the side of the lifeboat, so he hung on to Ferguson's neck and would not let go. "I hit him hard in the stomach with my elbow. He was wel-come to my spot at the rail; I wanted to leave there and strike out on my own." Ferguson became tired as he swam toward what he deemed to be a rescue ship; then, seeing a group of men about fifty feet away, he plunged toward them, hoping to rest himself a bit. "But when I got there I had to reach down so far to what they were holding . . . that the waves were washing over my head." He plowed on through the waves, swimming vigorously on the back sides and resting on the crests, conserving his strength in the process.[31]

This was Smith's first experience in the open waters of the sea. There is a huge difference, he maintains, "in what one views from the shore or from the deck of a ship, and being down there in the swells and waves." He, like many others, faced the danger of being sucked back into the ship's wake as she sank and the danger of the undercurrents, and he found himself inhaling and swallowing large quantities of salt water. He remembered, too, the strict rule of the convoy to preserve as many of its ships as possible when under heavy attack—even if that meant leaving injured survivors behind. If the convoy were so rigid in that regard, why, then, would any of the ships stop for someone out in the water? It was a desperately depressing thought, not only to Smith, but to hundreds of other men as well.

"I was on the verge of giving up because the mental strain was beginning to take its toll as was the physical exertion used to stay afloat and fight the waves," Smith recalled. Like so many other men, however, Smith heard an inner voice telling him that he could not give up, to keep fighting until there was no breath left in his body. Thoughts of his wife, Frances, began to flood his mind; thoughts of "how much her love and faith meant to me and how our religious beliefs and faith had given strength to our lives in the past." It had been difficult for Smith to leave his beloved wife, "but she had never shown that she ever doubted my returning to her." These thoughts strengthened Smith, enabling him to carry on.[32] But while his mental determination was in good shape, Smith's physical condition steadily deteriorated. The chill of the water—its taste and smell— and the oil-laden waves threatened to overcome him.[33]

Smith and many of these men reckoned themselves to be good swimmers, a belief that perhaps led dozens of them to shed their life belts so they could swim unencumbered—especially important if they saw a rescue ship in the distance. But since the rescue ships were constantly on the move, if a soldier saw one in a particular location and tried to swim toward it without his life belt, he usually became exhausted and drowned.

Inks, like many survivors, could not swim. He owes his life, he says, to God and a buddy named Leonard Deutsch. He helped Inks to get away from the sinking *Rohna* and then gave him the strength, encouragement, and stamina to hang on. "Leonard could swim," Inks recalls, "and possibly could have swum to a rescue ship . . . but he held back to assist me." Inks said the *Rohna* passengers had been instructed to stay in large groups if they ever had to go into the sea, "so as darkness descended we attached ourselves to the edge of a large floating mass of men," who supported themselves with their individual life belts and some hatch covers found in the water.

"I would estimate there were somewhere in the number of 100 to 200 men. Many were calm but there were some individuals who were determined to climb up onto the mass and ride it like a raft." With all the confusion and disorder here, Inks and Deutsch and a few of their comrades decided to leave the group and "take our chances." They "preempted" a couple of hatch covers and took off. They had no trouble staying afloat, although the sea was getting rougher by the minute. "One moment we were down in what seemed like a bowl and the next we were up on the rim, with the waves and spray hitting us in the face," making all of them "a little seasick from the motion and swallowing salt water."

What occurred next is something Inks still calls "the greatest and most memorable act of unselfishness and love for your fellow man that I have ever experienced." The group was quiet because of the waves and nausea. Deutsch then said to Inks, "Open your mouth!" Inks, not sure what he meant, replied, "What!" Deutsch repeated the order and quickly shoved a chocolate bar into Inks' mouth, giving him sustenance for this continuing ordeal. "That act," said Inks, "stands out in my mind more than any other detail of the disaster and has done much to shape my thinking about people who are of different religions, creeds, and origins." But apparently only one man from this group—Camdon Inks—was rescued; the others, because of the rough sea and the oil slick, were lost, including Leonard Deutsch. Inks says today: "Through the grace of God, the help and comfort of Leonard Deutsch and the able hands of the crew of HMS *Atherstone* I am a survivor of the *Rohna.*"[34]

But not all men cooperated with and helped each other; on the contrary, there were very few Leonard Deutsches in the water, since survival was uppermost in many men's minds. Finch, for example, came to a raft with men on board and hanging on. They refused Finch's entrance, and "one guy actually took a swing at me as I tried to catch the rope." Another GI, trying to get on the same raft as Finch, was brutally kicked in the face. He disappeared and presumably drowned.[35] Incidents like this did not indicate inherent "badness" so much as a basic, powerful instinct to stay alive.

Leaving the raft, Finch drifted alone, although he certainly could hear the screams and moans of men nearby, and every now and then a body bumped into him. One corpse stayed with Finch in the ups and downs of the water, "just as if he was lonely or something." His face, said Finch, was luminous in the blackness: "I could see it quite clearly even though it was pitch dark. . . . He stayed right with me wherever I went." Eventually the water and the body's presence overcame Finch, and he vomited. He took a drink of water from his dead companion's canteen and felt better, but it was not long until he became sick again. Then he felt dizzy and drifted off to sleep.[36]

James Lacy kept floating and swimming throughout the night. Whenever he spotted groups of men he swam over to them, only to find in each instance that all were dead. He finally hooked on to a group where some were still living. He owes his life, he believes, to a shipmate who suggested as he was abandoning the *Rohna* that he get rid of his heavy gear and take only his life preserver and a canteen full of drinking water. "You might want a drink of water tomorrow."[37]

Horton, drifting with an unknown man, also wanted a drink of water, but found he had no canteen with him, and his companion's was empty.[38] Indeed, there were many instances of—in the words of Samuel Taylor Coleridge's *Rime of the Ancient Mariner*—"water water everywhere, and not a drop to drink."

For the men of the *Rohna*, the sea was the great leveler. It did not matter if a man was enlisted, like Fievet, Finch, or Quick, or an officer, like Lieutenant Brewer, Dr. (Captain) Jackson, or Captain Murphy. There were no "officers'" or "enlisted" lifeboats or planks. There were no "high borns" or "low borns." All faced the same dangers, the same threat of death. Survival had nothing to do with rank—or a lack of it.

Throughout the ordeal, rescue ships, primarily from the convoy, had hovered in the vicinity, doing everything possible to pick up survivors. The *Pioneer* was foremost among the rescuing vessels, picking up two-thirds of all those who were saved. From 6:00 P.M. until after daybreak, the men on some of the ships that had been chosen for rescue duty worked as hard as they possibly could to save their comrades. For the most part, they succeeded admirably.

7

To the Rescue

GIs, 26 November: 6:30–9:00 P.M.

Well before convoy KMF-26 sailed into the
Mediterranean, its commanders had ordered
that, in the event of any sinkings, certain ships—
to be named at the time of the emergency
itself—would hold back for rescue work. In the
Rohna's case, the principal rescue ships were the
Atherstone, Holcombe, Mindful, Clan Campbell,
and minesweeper USS *Pioneer.* In addition, the
tug sent to tow the *Rohna* to port if she were salvageable played a small role in the rescue. The
sailors on board the rescue vessels felt it was
their personal responsibility to pull men from
the sea. In fact, many of the rescuers, anxious
to save as many men as possible, departed only
when they were ordered to do so by their super-

iors in Algiers. As daybreak neared on 27 November, there was the usual renewed threat from German aircraft and submarines, making timely departures essential. Nevertheless, the rescue ships managed to save all survivors within their sight and hearing.

The *Pioneer* was by far the most efficient of the rescue ships. After it was all over, the *Pioneer* had plucked 606 GIs from the Mediterranean; she stayed in the vicinity of the sinking *Rohna* until she was forced to leave, primarily because of excessive weight.

The *Pioneer* was commissioned on 27 February 1943, with Lt. H. B. Stevens assuming command. After her christening, she took her shakedown cruise in the Gulf of Mexico.[1]

The 890-ton *Pioneer* was 220 feet, 6 inches long; her beam measured 32 feet, and her top speed was 18 knots. She was armed with one three-inch 50-caliber gun, three 40-mm Bofors, and numerous machine guns. The crew consisted of 110 enlisted men and 12 officers; approximately 10 of the enlisted men were African-Americans, on board primarily to serve the officers' mess.

The ship arrived in Norfolk on 28 March, and by 3 April she was in Yorktown, where she took on fuel and supplies and began conducting exercises in minesweeping techniques. Then she steamed on to the Chesapeake Bay, where, outside of Annapolis, Maryland, she engaged in target practice, among her other exercises. On 20 April she was inspected by Adm. Ernest J. King, U.S. Chief of Naval Operations. Up and down the Potomac River the *Pioneer* continued her sweeping and gunnery training, preparing for her minesweeping tasks ahead.

Now under the command of Comdr. LeRoy ("Roy") Rogers, she left on 3 November for escort duty across the Atlantic. On the way, the crew continued the now routine sweeping and gunnery practices for everyone on board. On 16 November the *Pioneer* investigated possible enemy submarines coming toward her convoy, but—

The USS *Pioneer*, which rescued most of the *Rohna* survivors.

to the relief of all concerned—she came back with a negative report. It was during this escort voyage that the *Pioneer* was called on for special duty in November 1943, just one day after Thanksgiving.

On the morning of 26 November, the *Pioneer* was tied up at the pier in Bizerte, Tunisia. She had used this base (as well as one at Mers el Khebir, near Oran, Algeria) on previous layovers between voyages, carrying out sweeping and gunnery exercises and some short escort work. At about 8:00 A.M. that morning the *Pioneer* received orders to "get underway immediately"[2] and join KMF-26 as an escort vessel, replacing a British ship that had broken down. She was assigned a section on the port quarter of the convoy, and there she stayed throughout that fateful day. Though the men of the *Rohna* did not know her by name, the *Pioneer* was the first rescue ship most of them saw as they abandoned the *Rohna*.

Over and over the survivors recalled the high waves and rough seas that impeded the rescue operations. Some waves, they believe, were fifteen or even twenty feet high. One of the helmsmen of the *Pioneer*, however, says that the waves could not possibly have been that high, or the sea that rough, although there was a steady tide going out, away from the North African coast.[3]

He explains that, during the initial air raid on the 26th, he did his best to maneuver the *Pioneer* out of harm's way. "At no time did I have any problems with steering," he recalled. The *Pioneer* was a small ship; if the waves had been fifteen or twenty feet high, it would have been difficult, if not impossible, to rescue anyone because of the extra weight she took on as the survivors were brought on board. She could have been steered with little difficulty in seas as rough as the survivors claim, but she could not have laid to for any length of time; otherwise, she would have been swamped. Her freeboard (from the waterline to the main deck gunwale) was no more than nine feet. In the kind of seas the survivors described, the *Pioneer* would have rolled to such an extent that no one could have been lifted on board, and certainly no one could have gone over the side to assist those in the water.[4] The helmsman remembers that an Action Report coming from the USS *Portent* spoke of force-three winds—some fifteen miles per hour—which produced waves of five feet, with two and a half foot swells. "This coincides perfectly with my memory,"[5] said Wright.

The whole matter, of course, depended on perspective. The men on board the *Rohna* had been greatly traumatized well before they even left the ship. Also, "when you are in the ocean with anything over a six inch sea running you have a sight of the horizon not more than twenty-five percent of the time." Under these circumstances, five-foot waves can seem enormous.[6]

As Horton drifted and swam in these "mountainous" swells, he spotted a "little ship" about two hundred yards away, which turned out to be the *Pioneer,* and swam to it. He saw a large group of men around a ladder trying to grab on to its top rung. The *Pioneer* was rolling so much that if one had caught a lower rung, he would have been dipped back into the sea—a perilous possibility, especially if he lost his grip altogether. Horton, like many others, bided his time, and when the *Pioneer*'s deck rolled down close to the sea, he grabbed the next-to-the-top rung of the ladder and held on. Thus, when the ship rolled back, he had the momentum, after two sailors gave him a "helpful pull upward," to roll right onto the deck.[7] Diehl, too, "rolled" on board the *Pioneer* and found himself in the company of several cold, shivering men. "We were all wet and cold," he recalled, so they huddled together around one of the ship's stacks, which was issuing some heat. "I encouraged them to act like animals; like little pigs: you crowd in"; then once a man warmed up, he would "crowd out" to give someone else a chance.[8]

As soon as Schoenacker's head was above the deck line, strong arms grabbed him under each armpit, "and in one motion I was sent sliding on my backside across the deck." His head, shoulders, and back hurt from his ordeal in the water and from being hit with a floating object as he neared the *Pioneer.* A crew's mess had been turned into an emergency room. "Such a sight!" he exclaimed later. "The waiting injured sat dejectedly, the crew was working diligently in an ankle deep liquid with the consistency of water and the color of blood." Under the circumstances, Schoenacker never went into this room. Instead, he "forgot my pain" and went back on deck, hoping to help with further rescue efforts. But the crew told him they preferred that "I hide, not help." He found a small sheltered platform just outside the radio room, where he was essentially out of the way, although the radio operators had to step over him all through the night.[9]

Ferguson saw a man holding on to a line trailing out behind the *Pioneer*'s stern, but as he tried to join him, the man snarled, "I'm on here! I'm on here!" Ferguson grabbed the line anyway, but soon saw another line paralleling it about six feet away. He lunged for the second line, caught it, and began to work his way to the ship. He wrapped the line tightly around his wrist and tried to jump on board on the downward rolls. He was unsuccessful the first few tries, being battered up against the side of the *Pioneer* as she made a high roll. Ferguson apprehensively watched the two propellers, practically out of the water, "turning slowly in front of me." Finally a very large wave lifted him high enough to grab a support bar, which he learned later was holding a depth charge.

He placed one knee in the crotch of the support and then placed his foot on top of his knee. "I was ready to ride there indefinitely, but in a couple of minutes a crewman reached over the rail and helped me onto the deck." As Ferguson walked across the *Pioneer*'s deck, he saw the bodies of five comrades. Going down a ladder, he encountered other GIs, "all wet and tired looking." They cheered when they saw him; he was surprised, but soon found himself cheering also as others came down after him. "The camaraderie was so intense at that moment," he recalls, that "it is one of my most precious memories."[10]

Out in the water, as Peach approached the *Pioneer*, he listened as other men, despite having their mouths dried out and their tongues swollen by the salt water, shouted, cried, and moaned. It sent up a roar much like one would hear at a football game, except "instead of cheers men were crying out to God or the Holy Mother to save them." Peach grabbed a line lowered down the *Pioneer*'s side and tried to climb it. So many men clung to his waist, legs, and feet, however, that they all were plunged back into the sea. Peach was buffeted about and kicked in the head, at which point—despite his efforts not to—he panicked. He grabbed on to another soldier, who cursed him and punched him in the face. Peach laughed and apologized to the soldier, who quickly swam away. "He restored me to my senses."[11] Peach reconciled himself to the fact that he would have to remain in the water a while longer.

After what seemed an eternity, he saw a rope being lowered down the *Pioneer*'s side and frantically swam toward it. Two seamen pulled him up, telling him, "You're all right now; just come on over the side." Peach replied that he couldn't, since all his strength was gone, and he knew if he fell back into the sea, he would not make it. The sailors reached over and grabbed him and unceremoniously hauled him onto the deck, "like a wet flounder." He thanked his rescuers effusively, but they were too busy with other survivors to pay any further notice to him. Over and over Peach muttered, "Thank you God, thank you!"

One of the first persons Peach found on board the *Pioneer* was an old friend, Mike Vacca. The two embraced and wept with joy at being rescued.[12] Once they regained their composure, Peach mentioned that he badly needed shoes, since he had lost his during his ordeal. A sailor, trying to be helpful, pulled the cover back from five dead soldiers lying on the deck and said "take your pick." But Peach declined and decided to wait until they were on shore again.[13]

Peach and Vacca were led into a companionway, where other rescued men were lined up against the bulkheads. He saw one of his company officers standing "bone-dry" in his khakis and wearing his "go-to-hell" cap. He smiled and nodded at Peach; Peach responded "curtly" because, for unstated reasons, he had never liked this particular officer. Peach found Major Wagner, the man he had been walking with on the *Rohna* when the guided bomb struck. The major was eating a piece of pie, and suddenly Peach grew ill. Whether his nausea came from seeing the pie, ingesting huge amounts of salt water, or the ordeal itself is not clear, although it was probably a combination of the three. He apologized to the men around him, turned to the bulkhead, and violently vomited for the next several minutes. He believed he would feel better if he could get some fresh air and headed straight for the deck.[14]

One of the first things Miles saw after being hauled on board the *Pioneer* was a seaman sewing up a long rip in a soldier's leg. For anesthesia, the sailor gave the GI a "long slug" out of a liquor bottle. Miles recalled wistfully that the "soldier never complained of the pain!"[15] Caskey noticed a pharmacist's mate (whom the survivors forever called "Doctor")[16] treating the many wounded. There were some, he said, with "long black strings of skin hanging down from their bodies," presumably from oil burns they had suffered in the water. "Many were still yelling for their mothers, and praying. The ship was so over-crowded."[17]

As Red Cross man Sparks approached the *Pioneer*, he saw a light coming over his raft and heard a voice calling out from the darkness to "hold on for five minutes more!" For Sparks it was the longest five minutes of his life. All on Sparks's raft were saved, except for three men who were sucked under by the *Pioneer*'s propellers and mangled to death. Sparks's Red Cross colleague, Weinstein, spoke of an amber light hitting his eyes. "I thought for a minute I had really hit the gates of St. Peter," he said. Then someone called to him to grab the life preserver thrown to him. He could not get it on fully, for he found it impossible to unclamp his left hand from the oar he had been hanging on to for such a long time. Someone from the deck of the *Pioneer* "grabbed him by the hair" and pulled him on board.[18]

Everyone on Bronstein's lifeboat reached for the lines hanging from the *Pioneer*, but many were trembling so violently from cold that they either could not grab a line, or if they could, they could not hang on. Bronstein looked up and saw that he was near the lowest part of the ship and that there were "many heads and hands" extending toward him, all shouting for him to jump. He waited, however, until a big wave came along and lifted his lifeboat practically to the *Pioneer*'s deck. When his lifeboat reached the crest of a wave, he leapt and felt strong hands grasp him. "And so I was rescued."[19]

McKee, whose life belt had been pierced and was therefore useless, was, to the best of his recollection, in the water for about two hours. He swam with another GI with a functional life belt and reassured him that they both would be saved, "but as we got to the stern of the *Pioneer,* he left me to grab a 'bumper,'" a device that protects ships in port from serious damage from contact with one another. At that point, however, a huge upward roll occurred, causing the *Pioneer*'s stern to rise into the air. McKee's friend rose with it, and the ship then came down on top of him. "He was so close to being saved!" McKee grabbed a cargo net and hooked his leg through it; thus anchored, he spent the next hour or so pulling swimmers into the net, who then were lifted on board by *Pioneer* crew members. At last, overcome by the cold and exhaustion, McKee himself was pulled onto the minesweeper's deck, where he was immediately issued a blanket and ordered to go below,[20] since the *Pioneer,* by picking up so many survivors, was becoming top-heavy. Many on board predicted that she would not make it back to harbor. Bailey, for example, noted that when he came on board, her decks were "level with the water."[21]

Smith peered through the sea spray and dimly saw a ship approaching on his front right. At first he was elated, but then reality set in: How could anyone on a ship traveling that fast possibly see him? Nevertheless, he set himself a point where he—if he swam hard enough—and the ship would meet each other, but he missed; the vessel got to the imaginary point of contact before Smith and did not stop.

"Frantic would not describe my reaction," Smith recalled. The current carried him through the ship's wake, and he saw she was now on his left and behind him. Suddenly Smith saw the ship stop and begin drifting with the current. He used all of his energy, swimming against the current, and finally neared the starboard, or leeward, side—which at this point was the high side—but he could see no one on board. "Then the Good Lord sent a lone sailor around to my side of the ship," who threw a small white rope to him. As Smith neared the *Pioneer* a "fellow soldier came from nowhere," exhausted. Smith caught him by the collar of his coveralls and held him with one hand and the rope with the other; then "the sailor pulled us both to the side of the ship."

At that point, a large wave lifted Smith and his friend high, enabling the sailor to catch them both and pull them on board. "I remember that as I was pulled on the deck, my canteen hit the edge of the deck as my butt also made contact with the wet steel and the momentum carried me sliding across to the side of the smoke stack," in the center of the minesweeper. One of the first men Smith saw on board the *Pioneer* was an obnoxious officer who abruptly asked him, "Are you the sergeant I gave my life belt to?" Smith replied that he was not. "This made me feel very bad, in front of the men who, like myself, were in shock, while others were being pulled on board hurt and in pain. In my condition I almost lost my cool and was quick to let him know that I used my own life belt."[22] (Incidentally, Smith still has the life belt that he used in the Mediterranean).

At the time, Smith was gratified that the *Pioneer* apparently had stopped just for him. He found out later, however, that the reason he had not seen any men on the starboard side was that everyone had gone to the port side, where spotters had found a large mass of floating humanity. The ship had stopped to pick up those men who were still alive; it was "God's will" that the ship even stopped and that a lone sailor happened to appear on the portside deck and see Smith. He had always been a religious person, and this experience increased the faith that he already possessed.[23]

In another part of the sea, Hand climbed onto a hatch cover with thirteen other soldiers hanging on to it, and they floated for well over four hours. It was now quite late into the night, and no renewed German attacks were likely, nor had any enemy submarines been spotted. The Germans apparently had left the area. Hand therefore decided to use the flashlight he had brought with him. He ordered a few others to help him stand on the hatch cover, admonishing them, "don't let me fall off." He turned on the flashlight, and very soon a huge searchlight came from a nearby ship, signaling in code.

It was the *Pioneer.* One of Hand's companions was a signalman, who read the flashing lights. They were told to "hold on" for ten more minutes. Later, Hand was teased by his mates for "waiting for somebody from Texas"—the *Pioneer,* which was built in Beaumont —to pick him up.[24]

Finch remembered hazily seeing a ship in the distance that would come toward him one minute and turn away another, creating a surrealistic scene in the misty sea. Then a bright light—so bright that he "wished they would turn it out"—hit him in the face. Suddenly he was slammed up against the side of the ship he had been dreamily watching and was shaken "from head to foot," sharply bringing him back to reality. A rope hit him in the face and he tried to grab it with his left hand—his right hand was injured— but he could not hold on. A wave lifted the *Pioneer,* leaving Finch feebly hanging on to the rope in mid-air. He let go. "I was too well gone" to hold on. Then two sailors from the *Pioneer* jumped into the water and hung onto Finch as others on the deck hauled in all three. A large wave washed them onto the deck. "I was safe!" Finch remembered exuberantly. After his wounds were tended to, Finch went back out on deck, still in his wet clothes, where he stayed for the remainder of the night. "I was never so cold in my life," he said. (Half a century later, every time his "brain remembers" this ordeal, "I get cold again").[25]

Childress, long separated from his friend, Fievet, and floating with a large group, saw the *Pioneer* approach with her searchlights on; she then began to "scoop us up." He does not really remember being brought on board; he does recall, however, a sailor pumping saltwater out of him and saying that his body would not need any more salt for the rest of his life.[26] *Pioneer* crewman Clyde Bellomy gave respiratory treatment to another survivor, and when he came to, he told Bellomy, "Oh God, you're killing me." Bellomy was so glad to hear him talk that he told him, "Shut up or I'll throw you back."[27] Cunigan spent time going to the wounded and giving them shots of morphine to ease their pain. Like Bellomy, he gave artificial respiration to a rescued soldier. When the GI was recovered sufficiently, he told Cunigan to "get your big fat ass off; there ain't nothing wrong with me!"[28]

When Epifano reached the *Pioneer*, she was so low in the water that the African-American sailor who rescued him simply grabbed him by his pants and brought him on deck. He lay on the deck in a semiconscious state, but as the ship listed from side to side, he could see that many of those lying with him on the deck were dead, their heads flopping with the vessel's movements. Finally Epifano moved to the engine room, where it was warm; then a fellow survivor approached him and asked if Epifano by chance came from Cliffside Park, New Jersey. Epifano replied that he did and asked why this man wanted to know. It turned out that the soldier lived on Cliff Street in Cliffside Park; Epifano's residence was on Jersey Avenue, only two blocks away. The soldier had recognized Epifano from his old neighborhood days, but they had never actually met before this dreadful crisis.[29]

But while there were several happy reunions and many thankful survivors, there also were many men who died right at the side of the rescue vessels. Their rafts and lifeboats frequently were dashed against the ships and demolished, resulting in many deaths. The sea was rough, making it difficult for the *Pioneer* and most of the other rescue ships to lower their own boats. Many of these men from the *Rohna* had been injured when the guided bomb hit the *Rohna*, only to endure several hours in an unfriendly sea, hoping to be rescued. Too often they simply were too weak to climb on board, perishing on the very threshold of survival.

Also contributing to the fatalities were the large numbers of men clambering up the sides of ships. In their desperate efforts to get on board, some men pushed the heads of others under the water, causing them to drown. *Pioneer* crewman Ed Linville saw a soldier right beside the ship; a light was put on him, but he started sinking from exhaustion. "We could see him slowly going down in the water and moving his arms and legs ever so slowly." It appeared to those on deck that the young man had on a full field pack. Soon he sank out of the sight of the strong searchlight that had been beamed on him. "This I will never forget."[30]

But despite these incidents and the helplessness the rescuers often felt, they never gave up on the men in the water. Many men of the *Pioneer*, disregarding their own safety, went into the sea to help these *Rohna* survivors, displaying an almost missionary zeal to save lives. Without any orders or instructions, they dived over the minesweeper's sides to put life preservers over heads and under arms. When no life preservers were available, they tied lines around the swimmers and pulled them to the vessel's side so they could be lifted on board. With so many lives at stake, even the gunners left their stations to assist the deck crew. "Leaving a post during a battle," said Lt. Rogers, "is not considered a proper Navy procedure, but as C.O. they got no argument from me. I should have ordered it before they did it. I am very proud of all of them."[31]

Those who were saved have never forgotten the *Pioneer* seamen who tied ropes around their waists—as well as those who did not—and jumped into the water to help those without the strength to climb cargo nets, ropes, hoses, or any other object proffered to them. One particular seaman cited for his bravery was known for nearly fifty years in survivors' reports only as "the red-headed sailor." He turned out to be Harrell Jones, in charge of the *Pioneer*'s gunnery. "Jonesy," with a rope tied to his middle, stayed in the water for a number of hours, greeting the survivors, cheering them up, and getting them on board. Bellomy rescued many men as well, going into the water to save whomever he could, but, he later mused, "Old Jonesy was smarter than I was—he tied himself to a rope. That was a big help."[32]

Later on, sometime about mid-evening, Commander Rogers asked permission from naval authorities in Oran to leave the area.

Many men on board the *Pioneer* needed medical attention, some of them immediately, and the ship was listing badly from the weight of the extra passengers. Rogers' division commander denied permission and ordered the *Pioneer* to stand by for additional rescues. Rogers had all the searchlights turned on again, and the *Pioneer* continued to crisscross and circle the area.[33] Additional men were placed on spotting duty, enabling them to see and save several "late arrivers." Rogers later said that "somehow we stumbled through these activities" with only minor casualties. "It seems to me," he recalled, "that half the time I didn't know what the hell was going on, but somehow I had enough sense to stay out of the way of our crew, and let them run it. They did too, and for evermore, I'll consider myself the luckiest guy who ever went to sea."[34]

But it soon became clear to Rogers that he would have to leave, or run the real risk of destroying everything he and his crew had accomplished. But then, sometime around midnight, just as the *Pioneer* revved up her engines to prepare for departure, a spotter saw another *Rohna* survivor.

Out in the watery darkness, Zirkle had drifted by a captain who wore a luminous, waterproof watch. He told Zirkle that it was about midnight, a thought that cheered neither of them; it meant they had now been adrift for nearly six hours. Then a wave separated them. Zirkle then came upon a young man whose teeth were chattering so much that he could not talk but who kept throwing up saltwater. "Suddenly he just stiffened up and was dead." Zirkle drifted on into the night and finally saw a light in the distance and struggled toward it. It was the *Pioneer*. He found a hose hanging over the side and, with the help of a sailor who jumped into the water to assist him, Zirkle was brought on board.[35] He was the last *Rohna* survivor to be picked up by the *Pioneer*.

The first thing Zirkle heard when he got on board was Commander Rogers saying, "that's all. We're heading for shore." Zirkle turned to the "red-headed kid" (Jonesy?) who had pulled him from the water and said, "That's just like the military; it has to do every-thing by alphabetical order!" Zirkle happily drank strong coffee for the rest of the night.[36]

The *Pioneer* headed for shore—staggered is more like it—toward Phillipeville, in Algeria. She had 606 survivors on board (six of them died on the way to port). The average weight of each of these men was approximately 150 pounds, meaning the *Pioneer* now had an additional 45 tons to transport. This extra weight, added to that of the crew of 122 officers and enlisted men, put the minesweeper in a perilous situation. She absolutely had to leave the area, or else she, too, would become a casualty. Slowly she traveled, and the *Rohna* survivors finally began to realize that their hour of salvation was at hand. This long, horrible day of 26 November 1943 was now coming to an end. Never was there a greater sense of companion-ship than the one forged that night between the survivors of the *Rohna* and the *Pioneer* crewmen.

But it is important to remember that yet another three hundred *Rohna* survivors had been picked up by the other rescue vessels. Except for the small French tugboat sent out to tow the *Rohna* back to port if she were salvageable, the other rescue ships, unlike the smaller *Pioneer*, which could hold no more, stayed throughout the night. These larger ships found many clusters of floating men who had drifted steadily out to sea, away from the burning *Rohna*, and consequently far from the *Pioneer*. Often they were found several miles from the site of the sinking. Zielinski, for example, who was rescued by the tug *Mindful*, was found twenty-two miles away from where the *Rohna* sank. The water, he said, was so turbulent that men had to drift into the rescue ships themselves rather than the rescue ships approach them.[37] The *Holcombe*, *Atherstone*, *Mindful*, and *Clan Campbell* worked steadily throughout the dreary night, plucking men from the sea.

The corvette *Holcombe* dispatched a whaleboat to look for sur-vivors. After numerous unsuccessful attempts to attract rescuers' attention, Breedlove's group of floating men saw a searchlight moving in their direction around 2:00 A.M. "This time they heard our calls." The strong voice of a British sailor in the whaleboat told him to climb aboard, but he didn't have the strength to do so. The sailor then grabbed him under his arms and lifted him on board. He lay on the bottom of the boat while others were rescued; when the boat returned to the *Holcombe*, he and many of his comrades had to be carried on board. The sailors took Breedlove to the engine room, stripped off his clothes, and placed bottles of hot water between his legs and under his armpits. Then they wrapped him in blankets, and he soon fell asleep, warm at last. The ordeal was behind him. Later, he asked a British sailor how many of the thirty-two in his group had been picked up. He was told, sadly, that only five had been rescued.[38] The sailor also told Breedlove that they had picked him up about twenty miles from the site where the *Rohna* went down.

The destroyer *Atherstone* had at one time been the closest escort to the *Rohna*, but after narrowly escaping five guided bombs, she moved away from the convoy, guns blazing. After the *Rohna* had been hit, the escort commander (on board the *Pelican*) ordered the *Atherstone* into rescue duty.

Inks, floating with a group, suddenly was blinded by the lights of a ship that appeared to be right beside them. They had watched this ship for some time: She would turn on her lights long enough to spot survivors and then turn them off because of a continuing German submarine scare. Inks saw several men on rope ladders leading off the ship, down near the water, throwing out lines. Inks grabbed a rope, and by the time he neared the ship's side, the rope somehow had ended up around his neck. "I was fortunate not to be hanged," he later mused. He was semiconscious when taken from the water; soon, though, he was in a hammock in a warm compartment. He "passed out" until the following morning.[39]

Altogether, the *Atherstone* spent some nine hours rescuing survivors of the *Rohna*. Like the crew of the *Pioneer*, the *Atherstone* sailors frequently tied themselves to the ship with strong lines and went into the water, staying there until every possible survivor was on board. Later, Lt. Comdr. E. N. Wood of the *Atherstone* strongly recommended that each man on board a troopship be required to wear a strong belt or rope around his waist so that if he did have to be rescued from the sea, doing so would be greatly facilitated.[40] But nothing ever came of his recommendations.

Dr. Jackson, who never named the ship that rescued him, was able to place his raft at her side—after first being kicked away by frantic men trying to board her. Two sailors pulled him on deck and asked, "Can you make it now?" Jackson responded that he could, but he soon found that his legs were so stiff and cold that he was unable to move them; he had to lift them with his hands to get a firm hold on the railings. He was escorted to a hold in the ship where he was stripped of his clothing and given a hooded navy cape to wear. Then he went to a dining room, where he saw a young sailor treating the wounded as best he could. After Jackson quit shaking, he told the seaman he would take charge.[41]

He treated the bad burns with Vaseline. All he had for one man's scalp injury were compresses and a tight bandage. Another man with a scalp injury had a large flap of skin hanging down over his eyes. After searching, Jackson finally found enough sutures to sew the young man up. The victim had vomited on the deck, making it "as slick as ice," and to make matters worse, the ship was rocking, making it difficult for Jackson to maintain his footing. The navy cape he had put on was too big for him and cumbersome to the point of interfering with his work. He pulled it off and, completely nude, continued to operate on the soldier. "Everytime the ship rocked," he recalled, "the patient and I would slide all the way across the room and back." He finally got the laceration repaired, but he thought "it must have been a comical sight."

In addition to burns and scalp wounds, soldiers came in with broken fingers, arms, and legs. But for the most part Jackson treated men suffering from exhaustion. One soldier was brought to him, still alive but just barely breathing. Jackson performed artificial respiration, but to no avail. The young man died, and Jackson shoved his body under a bunk to keep him out of the way.

Another soldier was brought to the ship's galley who was "as crazy as he could be," grabbing the leg of a sink and not letting go. Jackson found a big butcher knife and cut off the soldier's clothes. When Jackson and his assistants got the young man's money belt, he violently resisted, grasping it with both hands, obviously thinking he was about to be robbed. Later, Jackson modestly said of the soldier: "He finally got all right."[42]

Once again facing exhaustion, Jackson and his assistants went to a small galley looking for something to eat. The only things to be found were hot tea and jelly sandwiches. For the rest of Jackson's life, he would say it was some of the best food he had ever eaten. He then went out on deck and saw several men in the water floating with their heads and feet under. They were not picked up because "only the ones that showed signs of life were picked up." Finally, Jackson knew he would have to get some rest; otherwise, he would jeopardize his work and his own health. He went to an officer's cabin and tried to sleep but found he could not. The cabin was much too hot, and he was still so nervous and restless that sleep would not come to him. So throughout the long night, Jackson alternated between trying to save the wounded and getting the much needed rest that continued to elude him.

The *Mindful*, like the *Atherstone*, stayed in the area until the early hours of morning, rescuing about two hundred men. Although she was larger than the *Pioneer*, she was still a small vessel, only a thousand tons, and frequently had been used as a tugboat. Perhaps it was the maneuverability of the *Mindful* and the *Pioneer* that made them more useful in rescue work than the much larger *Holcombe* and *Atherstone*. These smaller ships could get from one place to another in the increasingly swelling sea more easily than their heavier counterparts.

This maneuverability helped the *Mindful* eventually to reach Brewer, who had lost all concept of time as he drifted, always staying close to a large group but at the same time keeping his distance because he did not want to be pulled down by their struggles. Then they saw a light and swam toward it with renewed vigor. They could see men waiting on a deck, ready to throw lines and other equipment to them. Brewer grabbed a doughnut life preserver, put it around his neck, and headed for the stern of the ship, where the deck was closer to the water than the bow. But there he found dozens of men struggling, so he backed away from them. He rode in against the side of the *Mindful,* bracing his arms against the hull, and waited for a big wave. "Pretty soon one came along raising me a good ten feet up to the rail." He reached out and felt strong arms grasp him. He was thrilled to hear someone with a "distinct British accent" tell him, "Easy as you go there, lad." These were the sweetest words Brewer had ever heard.

But Brewer's legs would not work; the *Mindful* crew had to take him below, where they cut off his clothing and wrapped him in a warm blanket. They gave him a huge cup of hot tea, but he could not keep it down. The best thing he could do, he thought, was to pass out. As he slipped into unconsciousness, he "heard" Henrietta again, saying, "I told you that you could make it if you just tried."[43]

After floating an interminable time, Dr. Boone heard "a voice from the Gods" speaking to him in a "wonderful" British accent. "Ahoy there, who are you?" the voice asked. Boone responded with all the strength he had left. The British voice, however, replied, "We'll be back," and the ship disappeared, causing Boone to experience "utter helplessness" bordering on despair. The ship did return, however, and the English sailor and his mates threw cargo nets down for Boone and his companions to climb. One companion was in particularly bad shape, and when Boone's raft began to float away from the ship, he again was in imminent danger of drowning as the large waves swept over them. He finally was tied to a line and hoisted on board. Then additional lines were let down, and Boone and the other GIs wrapped them around their middles and wrists and were pulled upward. On board, they were treated to huge mugs of warm rum, followed by hot tea. "And all we asked for," said Boone, "was a cup of coffee!" Their wet clothes were removed and replaced with dry outfits, "and gradually we warmed, and the violent shivering which had consumed much of our energy abated."[44] In the wonderful embrace of deliverance, Boone and his comrades fell into a peaceful sleep. In the meantime, the *Mindful* kept up her work, rescuing many more. She left the area and headed for a North African port at approximately 2:30 A.M.

The *Clan Campbell* was primarily a cargo ship, running high in the water; therefore, her rescue capabilities were not as great as those of the other ships involved. Nevertheless, she gave a good account of herself, staying right along with the *Holcombe, Atherstone,* and *Mindful*—in fact, she was the last rescue ship to leave.

Hunter is one survivor who always will be thankful that she stayed so long. After what seemed to be a lifetime, he spotted a large ship with lights on and nets hanging over the side. He swam to her, grabbed a net, and started climbing while men on board simultaneously pulled it upward. Just when he got to the edge of the deck, his strength failed him completely, and he would have fallen back into the water had it not been for the two big arms that reached out and caught him. The crew of the *Clan Campbell* offered Hunter and his buddies dry clothing, dry beds, and "huge" drinks of rum "to get us warmed up."[45]

Mason saw the *Clan Campbell* as well and took hold of a cargo net, but it kept swinging widely with each roll of the ship. One second he was far out over the water; the next he was slamming into the hull. Just when Mason thought he would not make it, a British seaman climbed down the net, grabbed him, and pulled him the rest of the way to the deck. "He sat me down on the deck and after some words of encouragement he left saying that he had to try to help others."[46] In the end, the *Clan Campbell* saved eighty-three Americans in the aftermath of the *Rohna* sinking.

But there was at least one complaint regarding the work of the *Clan Campbell* crew. Pfc. Charles Crenshaw of the Army Air Forces said in his official report: "On the *Clan Campbell* there was no help from the crew; and the boys who were able had to help get the others on board."[47] A somewhat muted criticism of the *Clan Campbell* came from Army Air Forces 1st Lt. Robert D. Kruidenier: "The *Clan Campbell* had no extra crew members available to assist in boarding the ship."[48]

Dawn was breaking as the *Clan Campbell* began to make her way to Phillipeville (modern-day Skikda), on the North African coast. She arrived mid-morning on 27 November. As far as could be reasonably determined, there were no other men to be saved; besides, in daylight, this cargo ship would become extremely vulnerable to German submarine attacks; in fact, as an officer on board said, she would be a "palpably easy target for torpedoes."[49]

In the aftermath of the *Rohna*, it was suggested that ships like the *Clan Campbell* not be assigned to any kind of rescue service. Her freeboard—that is, the distance from the waterline to the edge of the first deck—was some thirty feet, or three times as high as the *Pioneer*'s. Many men were lost as they tried to climb on board. The *Clan Campbell*'s cargo nets became so heavy from water and men that the crew had to use winches to pull them up.[50] Moreover, there were not enough lines coming from the *Clan Campbell*, leading someone to suggest that if the ship were going to remain in rescue service, new lines with knots should be installed.[51] Less than a month after the *Rohna* tragedy, a message arrived from the *Pelican* "formally" detailing the *Clan Campbell* as a permanent rescue ship.

She was to be outfitted with new scrambling nets and lines, boats and rafts, and a full store of food and medical supplies "as requisite in case a trooper is sunk."[52]

On the morning of 27 November 1943, Americans were scattered on North African beaches all the way from Bougie through Djidjelli to Phillipeville. Emotions ran high because both the rescued and rescuers had just endured the longest night of their lives. Some, in fact, inspired by these strong feelings, later tried to capture their thoughts in poetry (see Appendix A).

To the personnel of the *Pioneer, Holcombe, Atherstone, Mindful,* and *Clan Campbell* must go the greatest accolades that can be given to seafarers. They did not simply rescue many survivors from the *Rohna*, they proved that they were willing to lay down their lives for their fellow man. It is an action that is part of the best tradition of sailors everywhere.

Chapter 8

Phillipeville and Beyond

Germans, 27 November: Occupied France

Although they did not sleep the night before, Dochtermann and his crew were up at first light, ready to fly the short distance to Merignac. The sky was overcast, but it was clear enough for the airmen to see. Taxiing on the runway at Merignac, Dochtermann spotted some of his colleagues waiting at the hangar in which his Heinkel 177 would be housed until the next sortie. Led by his squadron's first sergeant, Walter Kausche, the group was out in full dress uniform to greet the returning warriors. When their planes were safely inside the hangar, Kausche approached the crew with a large glass goblet in one hand and a huge bottle of champagne in the other. He filled the goblet and offered it to Dochtermann, congratulating him on his services to the Luftwaffe. Dochtermann took the goblet from Sergeant Kausche, but handed it to bombardier Zuther. After all, Zuther had guided the bomb to its target, and everyone agreed that he should take the first swallow. And amid the accolades of his admiring audience, he did.[1]

At the same time, the assembled German flight crews paid homage to their fallen comrades, who included Major Mons, the group commander, and Captain Hofmon, the group's adjutant. Dochtermann was happy, however, that all of the men who flew in his particular unit, including his own crew, came back unscathed.

With Mons's death, Dochtermann, as the most senior in service in KG II/Gruppe 40, should have been named the provisional commander—at least until a new, permanent commander could be named. Theoretically, he knew it had been his turn for a long time, but his superiors were of the opinion that he had not yet sufficiently proven himself. Their choice for new commander was Captain Rieder, who up until now had led KG III/Gruppe 40.[2]

Nevertheless, 27 November was a day of celebration for Dochtermann and his crew; they were alive and were being feted for their achievements against the enemy. Later in the afternoon, Dochtermann and his men indulged in some long overdue rest. They knew the next day would be quite busy.[3]

GIs, 27 November: North Africa

During the German celebrations, the *Pioneer, Holcombe, Atherstone, Mindful,* and *Clan Campbell* arrived at several North African ports. The *Pioneer* limped into Phillipeville at about 8:00 A.M. and disgorged her hurt, wounded, and dead. The *Holcombe* and *Atherstone* were not far behind, while the *Mindful* and *Hunt* (which joined the rescue efforts late and picked up a few men) made their way to Bougie. The *Clan Campbell* arrived at Phillipeville at around

2:00 P.M. The port cities of Phillipeville, Djidjelli, and Bougie became sites of great activity for the rest of the day, as exhausted GIs spread out up and down the white beaches.

The dead and wounded at Phillipeville (the "official" landing location) were driven by ambulance to the British 67th and 100th Hospitals. There were no American quartermasters in the area, so the able-bodied were met by English authorities and issued new temporary British uniforms ("right down to the hobnail boots,"[4]) until their own could be replaced, as well as shoes, blankets, tents, and food. "We assumed the appearance of British soldiers," Fievet remembered, "with everything but the accent."[5]

At Phillipeville, many of the men lacked the basic tools of hygiene, such as toothpaste and toothbrushes, and some did not have the funds to buy them. The Red Cross loaned each GI enough money for the basic necessities, but only if his commanding officer signed a note.[6] The Salvation Army, on the other hand, said Diehl, "supplied us with what we needed. I don't have a very good impression of the American Red Cross."[7]

When Caskey disembarked from the *Pioneer* early on the 27th, he and his friends were pelted with rocks by Arab youths. They did no real damage, but their actions simply added to the exhaustion, pain, and tragedy of their ordeal, leaving them feeling more isolated than before.[8] Breedlove as well encountered similar hostility. Numerous German sympathizers among the residents of Phillipeville shouted at him: "I am Nazi. Heil Hitler!"[9]

But more often than not the survivors encountered genuine kindness, especially from the nurses. One Scottish nurse at Phillipeville gave Caskey a heavy sweater, and Caskey has never forgiven himself "for not writing to her and thanking her" for her kindness.[10] Caskey's first meal in Phillipeville, courtesy of the British, was corned beef, which he recalled tasted "very good," especially after the "horrible food we had been given on the *Rohna*."[11]

Clancy was tended by two Scottish nurses, one of whom he called "Olive Oyl." She forced him to flex his fingers until the bandages on his hands were bloody. The other nurse was red headed and expressed a desire to go to America. The two young Scottish ladies brewed up the "most horrible cup of coffee" Clancy had ever tasted, but he drank it all, since it "was a special treat prepared by the tea drinking nurses for their 'yanks.'"[12] But perhaps Clancy's most vivid memory of Phillipeville is a lesson in heritage he learned during a conversation with a British soldier. Clancy had mentioned that his ethnic background was Irish; the soldier replied, "Really old chap; I thought you were an American." Clancy, abashed, "never made that mistake again."[13]

Schoenacker recalled standing at the head of the line for food and receiving C rations. "The first ones in line," he said, "got the pork and beans." He went to a tent where, after a while, a British soldier entered "looking for the Sergeant." Schoenacker asked which sergeant he meant, to which the ruddy Englishman answered, "The sergeant who wants beer." Schoenacker quickly assured him that *he* was the sergeant the soldier was looking for. Soon the young Englishman left with a dollar in his hand, leaving Schoenacker with three large bottles of strong English ale in his. Schoenacker and some friends then crossed the road to the beach and found a group of their comrades fairly drunk. Schoenacker somehow traded one of his English beers for a large bottle of Canadian Club. And "that is all I remember of Phillipeville."[14]

Smith walked shoeless off the *Pioneer* and onto the dock at Phillipeville. An officer told him where to find some shoes: back on board the ship. He returned to the deck, but saw only several dead men. When he realized what the officer had meant, Smith returned to the dock and told him, "I could not remove the shoes from a . . . fellow soldier and wear them."[15] Smith and several of his comrades then were taken a short distance up the coast to a Canadian camp, where they found their life belts and canteens, which had been strewn along the roadside by the *Pioneer* crew. The men were taken to large supply tents, each of which housed thirty or forty men. There were no individual bunks; each man was issued a blanket, and he slept on the floor. But no one complained about these accommodations, said Fievet. "After floating in the Mediterranean, we welcomed the hard solid ground."[16] Sleep, however, was hard to come by: "We were so exhausted and down that sleep was fitful." Smith does not even remember any of the meals he had while in his tent on the shores of the Mediterranean. "We had no mess kits or anything to eat with." But more worrisome than this was the anxiety Smith and his buddies felt about their families back home. What were they being told, they wondered. There were no American officers in the Canadian camp, so Smith had no way to get word to his family that he was safe. Even if there had been an American present, Smith's family still would not have been notified of his circumstances because of the strict cloak of secrecy the American and British governments had placed around the sinking of the *Rohna*.[17]

Another survivor, Kroog, went to a Scottish medical encampment, where he found that he had lost some teeth—"only the roots were left."[18] After his teeth, as well as numerous chest burns and cuts, had been treated, he walked along the shore back to camp and was stunned to see several dozen men swimming out in the Mediterranean and seeming to enjoy it![19] One of these men was Horton, who needed to prove to himself that he was not afraid of the water. Yet another sight Kroog encountered along these beaches was thousands of bills of various denominations being dried in the sun.[20] Indeed, out in the water many men reported seeing huge sums of money floating by them—money from the marathon poker and dice games that had taken place on the *Rohna* and in the camps where the men waited for embarkation.[21]

The men of the *Rohna* had the "R&R" they needed for the next several days in Phillipeville and enjoyed it, with two exceptions: The unit commanders were ordering them not to talk about the *Rohna* incident even among themselves. These men knew that if the U.S. government didn't want them speaking of it, their families at home certainly would know nothing of their whereabouts. It was a troubling thought: Families stateside would begin to wonder why they weren't hearing from their sons and husbands. In many instances, they didn't learn anything until these GIs were in the China-Burma-India (CBI) theater, and even then any reference to the *Rohna* was carefully excised by military censors. Second, the men had to endure the heart-rending roll call of the 853rd Aviation Engineer Battalion. Out of 793 enlisted men, only 129, or some 13 percent of the battalion, were there to answer the morning roll call on 27 November.[22] Many of the survivors asked themselves why they survived and so many of their friends and comrades were lost. This question haunted many of the survivors for the rest of their lives.

(On 31 December 1943 survivor rosters were more complete than they had been on 27 November. Of the 30 officers and 793 enlisted men of the 853rd who had boarded the *Rohna*, 10 officers were missing in action, as were 485 enlisted. Of the survivors, 9 officers and 138 enlisted were injured. The 853rd had lost 62 percent of its personnel.)[23]

At Bougie, survivors, like their counterparts in Phillipeville, were met by British personnel, who lodged them in large tents and supplied them with clothes, toiletries, shoes, and uniforms. Some were taken to hospitals where for several days they rested and had their various injuries treated. Lacy recalled being treated well at the British Army hospital at Bougie, but the nurses kept waking him to see if he wanted tea and crumpets. After a week in this hospital, he went to the morgue—where clothing and boots from various sources, including British and American uniforms from Operation Torch the year before, had been stored—to collect clothes from the clerk there.[24]

Dr. Jackson had been suffering from a cold even before the *Rohna* left Oran, and now, after his ordeal, he was dangerously tired. He was admitted into another Bougie hospital.[25] "I was tucked into bed by a nice British sister or nurse. A pair of long, red knitted socks were put on me and I was placed in a good warm bed with a hot water bottle with a red knitted jacket on it." After a cup of hot tea, the nurse administered a dose of dovers powders (a mixture of opium and ipecacuanha), and Jackson soon fell into a peaceful sleep. For the next several days, Jackson greeted each morning with a big cup of hot tea and a mug of Guinness beer, but he later admitted he did not care for the beer.[26]

As the *Rohna* men recovered in North Africa, search teams continued to look for other survivors, although the official cutoff date for locating survivors was 27 November 1943. Officials cited the experiments—conducted throughout the war—of Lt. Col. George H. Holt in rescue missions in the Gulf of Mexico, the Pacific, and the Atlantic as conclusive evidence that no one in the water could have survived through 27 November. Holt believed that a person "in perfect physical condition and possessed of the highest possible degree of stamina could not possibly survive immersion in water of 60 degree temperature for a period in excess of 24 hours unless equipped with special protective clothing."[27] But despite this official stance, the search area was widened to include all territories of the Mediterranean from Spanish Morocco in the west to the coast of Palestine in the east. No survivors were found.

What the searchers did find, however, caused many to lose several nights' sleep. On 28 November, an American freighter, the *Andrew Hamilton*, passed through the search area and "plowed" through the bodies of many American soldiers floating in the Mediterranean. "At least 50 bodies close by the ship were counted in a period of about 15 minutes. The soldiers were fully dressed and wore life preservers."[28] But the *Andrew Hamilton* could not stop to recover any bodies; it had orders to steam onward toward the east.[29] On 2 December an air squadron out of Bone, Algeria, reported: "Approximately 25 miles off coast Bougie, Algeria, . . . bodies in water fairly close together in groups 150 to 200 traveling east at 2 miles per day."[30] By this time, however, all searches for survivors had been called off, as well as all efforts to recover bodies. Over a month later, on 10 January 1944, searchers sighted the body of a U.S. soldier washed up on the beaches of Italy. "His body was in an advanced state of putrefaction and was minus legs from the knee down and his skull was already a complete skeleton." He was identified through his dogtags and Social Security card as a young man from Kentucky. More and more of these reports were received during the remainder of 1943 and well into 1944.[31] Sometimes bodies were identified through tattoos or markings on fatigues, shorts, and undershirts. Many had written their names into the inner linings of their jackets and trousers.[32]

By now, the U.S. commanders in Algeria and Adjutant General's office in Washington, D.C., knew that steps had to be taken to see that U.S. Public Law 490 was complied with in the *Rohna* case. This law provided that all military personnel reported missing in action would remain in that status for twelve months unless absolute proof were given in the meantime that such personnel had shown up alive somewhere or were positively known to have perished. About 80 American bodies eventually were recovered from the sea; the remaining 829 missing (827 troops and 2 Red Cross workers) were declared after approximately a week to be "unrecoverable." Consequently, the U.S. government fixed the date of death for these men as 27 November 1943, with 5 May 1944 given as "the date conclusive evidence of death was received by the Secretary of War" in Washington.[33] But a report from the Mediterranean Theater of Operations dated 25 January 1946 noted that errors had been made in recording the time of death for numerous *Rohna* victims. The 27th of November 1943 was given as the date of death for most of them, but transcription errors caused the official date of death for eighty-six of these men to be given as 27 November *1944,* or exactly a year and a day after they actually died.[34] Some of these errors were left uncorrected for several years, and some probably are still incorrect to this day. Clearly such mistakes were not intentional, but months, or even years, later, when the victims' families became aware of the errors, they concluded that the U.S. and British governments had been far too negligent about the destruction of the *Rohna* and the loss of their loved ones.

On the whole, however, the record of troop transport in World War II generally was quite good. The War Department claimed that 4,453,061 American soldiers were transported to Europe during 41 months of war. Out of this number, 3,604 were lost at sea— 1,015, or roughly one-third, came from one ship, HMT *Rohna.*[35]

Germans, 28 November: Conferences and Trophies

While the survivors of the *Rohna* were recuperating along the beaches from Phillipeville to Djidjelli, 28 November was another early day for Dochtermann. He had celebrated the day before; now he was scheduled for numerous "debriefing" sessions, review conferences, and additional accolades from his comrades. All the members of his unit met to discuss what had been learned in the attack on KMF-26, particularly in tactics and timing. They spoke about possible improvements in the bomb's steering mechanisms and about permitting each plane to take along three Hs 293s instead of two in future attacks. (Although the planes had been outfitted to carry three bombs—one under each wing and one under the fuselage—it was believed that weight factors dictated against the practice.) Sitting in on these discussions was an interested Gen. Herhud von Rhoden of the German Luftwaffe operations staff. An important part of these conferences was to draw conclusions and consequences from Dochtermann and his crew's experiences and insights for future guided bomb attacks.[36]

A few days after this meeting, Dochtermann and his crew were ordered to Gen. Johannes Fink's command post near Istres, France, to represent their squadron in still more lengthy discussions of the attack on KMF-26. Numerous commanders of other fighter squadrons were present, including the leader of Torpedo Squadron KG 26 (who had much experience with Heinkel 111s) and a commander of a long-range reconnaissance unit, all of whom were anxious to hear about the dawning of guided-bomb warfare. Dochtermann and his men provided vivid descriptions—giving the minutest details of what they had done and experienced—and clear, sober, and objective explanations to their fascinated audience.[37]

When it came time to pass out the trophies, however, disagreements arose about protocol and justifications, to Dochtermann's disappointment and anger. General Fink was a time-tested veteran of the *Luftwaffe* who had seen action on the western front, particularly in the blitz against England. "Far be it from General Fink," Dochtermann sarcastically remarked, "to exercise unjustified criticisms about our squadron." Fink used his influence with various government offices to set up a "hierarchy" of prizes and awards when it came to applying for distinction in the attack on KMF-26.

The Iron Cross, second class (EKII) was awarded to all squadron members who had not yet received any distinction for bravery. The Iron Cross, first class (EKI) went to all those who had received an EKII in the past. The Cup of Honor, or *Ehrenpokal* (which existed only in the Luftwaffe), for special achievements in the air war, was awarded to all EKI bearers. The German Cross in Gold was awarded to all those who already had the Cup of Honor.[38]

The Cup of Honor, made of silver, was large enough to contain the contents of a large bottle of champagne. (In the course of the war, however, as silver was used increasingly for the German war effort, the honor was given in the form of a written certificate and an assurance that the cup would be handed out at the end of the war—but recipients never received them.)

Dochtermann already possessed the EKI (awarded on 27 June 1940); thus, his squadron recommended that he be given the Ehrenpokal. The application was denied, however, on the grounds that the sinking of the *Rohna* did not meet the requirements, because it was only the first "big blow" Dochtermann had, and his superiors expected more. Only with further successful missions could a new application be made for the most coveted award of the German flyer. Dochtermann eventually did receive the Cup of Honor on 30 March 1944—in the form of a written certificate.[39]

Several days after the award ceremonies, Dochtermann was ordered to appear at Schwabisch Hall for a meeting with General Heyn, the section commander of the "fighting pilots" (*Kampflieger*— an organization that was a part of the aerial ministry of the Reich) and directly under the command of Reichmarshal Hermann Goering. At this time, in late 1943, Lt. Col. Werner Baumbach was chief of the Kampflieger and earlier had been distinguished with the "swords on the Knight's Cross of the Iron Cross" for his individual successes against ships in convoy. "From his own experiences," said Dochtermann, "he knew what it took to attack convoys."

But the meeting between Heyn, Dochtermann, and Baumbach did not go well. "We didn't exactly expect hymns of praise" from Baumbach, said Dochtermann. "But we also hadn't expected that he would bring a message from the Reichsmarshal to shit on us."[40] According to Goering and Baumbach, the attack on KMF-26 and the sinking of the *Rohna* "had been a complete failure effectively to utilize the weapon HS 293." After all, most of them had missed. Only one had scored.

Such an "armchair judgement" took Dochtermann's breath away. He recovered quickly, however, and recklessly suggested that "in case the Reichsmarshal [Goering] should speak" to Baumbach again on this subject, "please convey to him that he ought to be proud that he still has flyers who approach the enemy with such unconditional courage, despite the strongest air defenses" against them.[41] He considered Goering's and Baumbach's attitudes as sheer ingratitude for what he and his crew had done. It would be several years before he could reconcile himself to these criticisms.

GIs: 40s and 8s

The problems Dochtermann faced in getting a medal paled in comparison to those confronting the *Rohna* survivors. Almost every GI had lost his personal papers, and it sometimes took weeks, even months, for them to be fully restored. Everything about the soldier, including his experiences on the *Rohna*, had to be reconstructed, and in the process, mistakes were made by the GIs and the army recorders, as well as the War Department itself. On 29 January 1944, for instance, a memo from the Adjutant General's office stated, "Because of the fact that no United States naval vessels were included in the escort, it will be necessary to contact the British Admiralty to obtain an official report of the circumstances surrounding the sinking of the "ROHNA.""[42] Surely the personnel of the *Frederick C. Davis, Portent, Herbert C. Jones*—to say nothing of the *Pioneer*—would have been surprised to learn that no American vessels were in the convoy. Since the *Rohna* was a British ship, most of the logs and descriptions regarding 26 November 1943 were housed in England. And a strict cloak of secrecy on the part of the American and British governments would keep anyone from seeing those records for years to come. Many commendations were not made simply on the grounds that the paperwork would be too horrendous. In later years, unless the GI himself collected documentation, nothing more was done toward recognizing his services to his country.

The family of Russell Cherry was notified that he had been wounded on board the *Rohna*, but he never received any type of medal from the government.[43] Bailey, also injured on board the *Rohna,* applied for a pension at the end of the war. But there was no record of his injury; there was no record that he had not been paid for the month of December 1943. In fact, the Veterans' Administration could find no record of a sinking on 26 November 1943. Bailey finally shrugged it all off. "You just drop it and say it's the government."[44]

There were, however, at least two hundred Purple Heart medals handed out to those wounded on the *Rohna,* most of them awarded to the 853rd Aviation Battalion. On 26 November 1944, at Kalaikundah, India, 133 Purple Heart medals were awarded. (And apparently the U.S. military still operates strictly alphabetically: Zirkle received his medal on 30 April 1994. It was presented to him during a family gathering by Brig. Gen. Thomas Neary at Warren Air Force Base, Wyoming. In attendance were two of Zirkle's great-grandchildren. But, he said, there were "many years of fighting with the Veterans' Administration" to prove that HMT *Rohna* had *ever even existed*).[45]

But in late November 1943 in North Africa, trophies, medals, and paperwork were far from the thoughts of the *Rohna* survivors. As they continued to recover in Phillipeville, Djidjelli, and Bougie, they worried about their families, what their next assignments would be, whether their units would stay together (there was talk that they would be split up and assigned to many different battalions), and how to cope with the daytime tremors and nightmares— where they relived the tragedy over and over—that were becoming commonplace. In fact, for many, these nightmares persisted for decades after the war. Many of the men also suffered from emotional stresses and anxiety attacks,[46] asking why were they saved while so many of their comrades had been lost at sea.

In spite of this, by mid-December 1943, the commanders of the *Rohna* survivors declared that the men were ready to move out of Phillipeville, Bougie, and Djidjelli and resume their journey to India. They began the trip on a quaint little train that ran on a narrow gauge. For many years in colonial Algeria, the "40 & 8" railcars had been used by French military personnel. The "40 & 8" had become quite well known to American soldiers during World War I. The "40/8" designation meant the car could hold 40 men and 8 horses.

The train started out at Bougie and worked its way through Djidjelli and Phillipeville, stopping for a while at Bone, on the way to Bizerte, Tunisia. Each car held about twenty men and was furnished with a case of C rations as a supplementary food supply. There were no toilets; a man had to relieve himself as the train moved slowly through the countryside or stopped at a siding.[47] Many times when the train came to a high grade all the men would get out and run alongside it. They used these opportunities for toilet calls, gathering firewood, and exercising. Right at the top of the hill, just before the downward grade, everyone hustled back aboard.[48]

For heat, each car was equipped with half an oil drum, in which the men kept a fire burning with the sticks and straw found along the way. One coach was designated the "kitchen car," although meals were served irregularly on this three-day trip. At mealtime the train stopped, and each man went with his mess kit through the line to find a place to eat. Powdered eggs and potatoes were the general rule during these mealtimes. Since the train did not travel at night, the men bedded down crosswise in the cars, each with a blanket. As they fell asleep, they could see the snow atop the distant mountains. Childress remarked, in understatement, "This made for a memorable trip."[49]

The men watched, spellbound, as the countryside moved slowly past them, "strewn with evidence of the recent fighting that had taken place by the Allied Armies in driving Rommel's forces from North Africa."[50] They saw hundreds of burned out trucks, tanks, and troop carriers that had once belonged to the Americans, British, and Germans. "These sights did not boost our morale."[51] Because of the damage done to the railroad, there was no direct route to Bizerte, resulting in long layovers on sidings, especially at night. "Whenever the train stopped or slowed down to its usual slow speed during the daylight hours, the Arabian hucksters, beggars, and children would be at the doors."[52] On the positive side, however, at each stop crowds of Frenchwomen congregated and sold or otherwise bartered large quantities of wine,[53] and on some very welcome occasions loaves of freshly baked bread.

At the stopover in Bone, Lieutenant Brewer located an American supply camp and tried to get U.S. uniforms for himself and some of his men. "The officer in charge seemed to think we were imposters rather than shipwreck survivors. He threatened to throw us in the stockade!" After much persuasion, the supply officer checked their story with U.S. authorities in Algiers. Yes, there had been a ship named *Rohna*. Yes, the men he was dealing with were American survivors. "We were then treated more respectfully and issued clothing and U.S. currency."[54] Most of the men on the train, however, had to wait until their arrival at Bizerte before being issued new U.S. uniforms and money.

Bizerte, a heavily bombed Tunisian city, became home for the *Rohna* survivors for the next few weeks. First, they were issued American uniforms, many of which were used—taken from dead soldiers who had fought in the North African campaign.[55] Second, their records had to be reinstituted, which was an arduous, time-consuming job plagued by omissions and incorrect information that would give many of these men "redtape headaches" for years to come. Third, despite the fact that it was the middle of winter, they were assigned to "tent city," a large conglomeration of temporary structures in an olive grove, each occupied by four men. They warmed themselves as best they could with stoves made out of five-gallon cans, using shell casings as stovepipes.[56] Jackson's stove was made of an old oil drum; he used old motor oil as fuel. Sometimes the stove smoked; "sometimes [it] would blow up."[57]

Rain fell almost constantly, and occasionally it snowed, making the camp muddy and even colder. Nevertheless, many men, particularly the officers, made frequent trips into the city of Bizerte. One lieutenant found a British lorry—he and his friends called it the "Bouncing Bitch"—and, since it was not otherwise being used, hauled many of his friends—despite its right-hand steering wheel—into the city and around the countryside. Jackson (who had been driven by British lorry from Bougie to Bizerte) said that "we used the truck to do all our running around in. We saw a lot of the country that we could not have seen if we hadn't had this truck."[58]

At the same time the men were enjoying themselves in their recovery, there were persistent rumors of "reorganizing" all these GIs into other groups. Lieutenant Brewer tells what happened: "Eisenhower's headquarters wanted us to go to Italy, and we were kind of thrown to the four winds, and fortunately we persisted in trying to get word over to our units in India that we were coming. We would get scattered chances to get message notices on them. Other survivors were good with the code key and finally we did get the word . . . to Colonel Jesse Guthrie that we were alive and we were coming and we had managed to save our shipment number headed his way."[59] Guthrie, in turn, pressured the military hierarchy; as a result, most of the units that had been on the *Rohna* remained intact and ultimately went on to India.

When the time came to depart, the *Rohna* survivors heard much activity around them as men and materiel were amassed for the upcoming campaign in Italy. The men knew this confrontation had first priority with the commanders, and they were proud to be defending their country; still, they felt slighted, believing that their superiors were not seeing to their mental, emotional, and religious needs as fully as they should have. "Some of our fellows were in pretty bad condition mentally and emotionally. Some could not sleep, some could not eat or relax. We were never debriefed or visited by a chaplain. It was a matter of a fellow soldier taking care of a fellow soldier."[60]

The men spent Christmas day 1943 at Bizerte, burning green olive wood in their makeshift stoves and "missing close buddies who had not made it."[61] The day before, Jackson and several friends had gone into Bizerte to take hot baths. Then they went to an officers' club, accompanied by Colonel Frolich, commander of the 853rd, "and we all got pretty tight."[62] Later that night they returned to camp and sang Christmas carols well into the night, going around to each tent with a candle. "A fellow had to do something to take his mind off his troubles."[63]

Clancy and a dozen or so of his comrades went to Midnight Mass at a small Catholic church on the top of a cliff overlooking the Mediterranean Sea. As they limped and hobbled out of the truck with their bandages, slings, and crutches, every civilian in the chapel got up from their seats and offered them to the GIs.[64] Caskey and five of his buddies spent all of Christmas eve in the foyer of another Catholic church, since that was "about the only thing left of the church." Just outside, a partial cockpit of a German plane was lodged in an olive tree.[65]

During this time, back in Salinesville, Ohio, the family of Eugene Brown received a Christmas card depicting a wizened old man with gifts riding a donkey and an exuberant GI hitching a ride behind him. The caption read:

By Christmas time as you can see
  There ain't no telling where I'll be.
But if I can find the transportation
  or other means of communication
You should receive this friendly word
  From the guy you know in the 853rd.

At about the same time, the card the family had sent to Eugene Brown was returned unopened, with the stark notice on the front that Brown was missing in action as of 26 November 1943. His body was never recovered from the Mediterranean.[66]

In Johnstown, Pennsylvania, Milford Bowden's family experienced the same grief. His Aunt Ida had written Christmas greetings to him—not knowing about the events of 26 November—"I hope you are well and guess we can't wish much of anything else for you for Christmas. But we will hope you boys are all home before another Christmas. . . . I hope this mess will soon be over and you will be home."[67] Her letter later was returned, with the message "Missing in Action" and the signature of 1st Lt. Charles Beard written on the envelope. This was the first anyone in Milford's family had heard of his fate.

In October 1943, Pvt. William Casilio of Pittsburgh, Pennsylvania, was given emergency leave to attend his brother's funeral; he had to leave the next day to rejoin his unit in Newport News, Virginia. "That was the last day we saw him too," his sister Angeline said many years later. "We never got any of his mail or our mail until he was missing in action."[68] Casilio had been lost in the attack on the *Rohna*.

During the long layover at Bizerte, time lay heavy on the mens' hands. They played cards and dice, read books, wrote home, and occasionally penned a few poems (see Appendix A for the text of these poems). Consequently, they were pleasantly surprised on New Year's Day when the *Pioneer* pulled into harbor. "What a great reunion we had with them!"[69] Someone found an old German jeep, repaired it, and went on a "mercy mission" to Tunis to pick up some liquor; a great celebration followed.[70] "We had a tent full of booze," said Finch. He told Wayne Dana, a member of the *Pioneer*, that with the liquor they could buy and steal in Tunis, "we had a truckload." Finch himself had acquired a German jeep from an Arab in return for a P-38 pistol. "Some of the navy guys were fooling with the jeep" when somehow it slipped out of gear and "ran down a little hill" directly into an officers' tent. "They took the jeep and I never did get it back. We left there a short time later, anyway."[71]

Finally, on 8 January 1944, the men were taken to the port of Ferryville, near Bizerte, to board a ship (part of a three-ship convoy) and resume their trip to India. The ship was the *Takliwa,* and it was almost an exact replica of the *Rohna*—even down to the type of lifeboats, life rafts, and Indian crew.[72] Some of the officers knew that the *Takliwa* had been attacked on 11 November 1943 while sailing in a convoy from Oran to Algiers.[73] As a result, there was a near-riot when the men saw the *Takliwa,* and talk of mutiny was in the air, as several GIs at first said they would not board her.[74] The men eventually did board, but they insisted—and their officers agreed—that they be put in charge of the lifeboats, life rafts, and the necessary operating equipment. It took them only a few hours to learn the routine, after which they relieved the lascars of these duties.[75]

Their first port of call was Port Said on the Suez Canal, and they were pleasantly surprised to see the *Banfora* anchored out in Lake Ishamalia. Lt. Col. John Virden, who had been the press officer on board the *Rohna,* and about twenty other survivors—some still with arms in slings and others on crutches—boarded the *Banfora.* The *Rohna* men were pleased when they found that many of their own footlockers were in fact on board, so some fortunate men "had not lost everything after all."[76] (As it turned out, back at Oran, the "baggage smashers" had felt that since all the ships would end up in the same place anyway, it did not matter if passengers and their footlockers were occasionally separated.)

After a pleasant reunion, the men of the *Rohna* continued on to Bombay. The voyage took approximately thirty days, and after the men got over their initial fears, it turned out to be a rather enjoyable experience. They were alerted to some Japanese submarine activity in the Red Sea, but nothing came of it. In early February 1944 they arrived in Bombay, refreshed and for the most part ready for action—action they would see in the CBI Theater.

Chapter 9

Welcome the Travelers Home

News Blackouts

Each side, of course, had its own version of what happened. A few days after the attack on KMF-26 and the destruction of the *Rohna*, the British Broadcasting Corporation (BBC), in its "Germany Calling" program, exuberantly announced that, according to eyewitnesses, the plane from which the fatal bomb had been fired was shot down. The Germans certainly were amazed to hear this report; they knew both the British and American governments would in no way reveal to their own publics what had actually happened. (And to this day, many survivors of the *Rohna* believe that the offending plane was, in fact, shot down).

One interested listener of BBC's "Germany Calling"—broadcast entirely in German—was Dochtermann himself. He was most surprised to hear that he had been shot down. He is not sure why such a report was made, but he believes it was because, before the guided bomb was released, he had maneuvered his plane first at high speed and then low speed, causing a great deal of carbon to build up on the exhaust pipes of his engines. When he went into the nosedive just after firing the bomb, the heat was so intense that it burned off all the carbon that had accumulated on the engines, creating a large, black cloud of smoke. To those below, it certainly must have appeared that he had been hit and was crashing headlong into the Mediterranean.[1]

But such misinformation was not exclusive to the British. The Germans, either from insufficient information or deliberate miscalculation, distorted several substantial facts themselves. Early war reports for 26 November 1943 revolved around the "terroristic" bombings of places like Bremen, where some of the bombs hit a hospital. But a German report of 28 November noted that "two destroyers and three troop transport ships" had been destroyed in KMF-26, while three others had been seriously damaged.[2] Two days later, the reports were changed, stating that *four* ships in a convoy that was plying its way eastward through the Mediterranean had been destroyed.[3] Altogether, these various reports maintained that some 140,000 tons of Allied shipping had been destroyed or damaged.[4]

One German newspaper spoke directly of the attack on KMF-26 and the destruction of the *Rohna*. The Americans, it said, had no idea why they were fighting Hitler's Germany, instead of "aggressors" like Britain and Russia. The article then concluded that, due to their own ignorance, the American and British men killed probably deserved their fates. Though the Germans did not know the name of the ship they had destroyed that day, this report noted that literally hundreds of "seasick" GIs converged on the deck, where for several minutes there was pandemonium.[5]

Clearly the Germans wanted the news about the power of their guided bomb, as demonstrated by the sinking of the *Rohna*, to spread as quickly as possible. Equally clearly, the British and Americans wanted to keep it strictly secret—so much so that top officials ordered all survivors to say nothing about the incident in their letters (when they were actually able to write) to relatives back home. One English seaman, James S. Thompson, ashore at Bizerte, apparently asked too many questions about the event. He was visited by an American military police officer "who advised me that if I had heard anything [about the *Rohna*] not to talk of it, and best of all to forget it."[6]

For some time after the tragedy, Lieutenant Brewer kept writing V letters to his wife and family back in California, primarily to let them know that he was alive. (A "V" letter was a very thin sheet of paper; one wrote on one side and addressed the other, then folded the ends together and glued them shut. They were called V letters because not much wood product was used in manufacturing them, thus contributing to the U.S. victory of World War II.) Anything that remotely hinted at the destruction of the *Rohna* and its aftermath, however, was carefully excised by the censors. The Army, citing military security, did not release the death toll from the disaster until well into February 1944, and even then it refused to name the ship or give any details of the sinking.[7]

This official secrecy undoubtedly is why Mrs. Anita Guidry, of Cut Off, Louisiana, and her three sisters had to wait over fifty years to find out the circumstances of the death of their brother, Livingston Collins. The War Department had sent a telegram dated 27 December 1943 to his mother, Marie, in Goldenmeadow, Louisiana, saying that he had been missing in action since 26 November. Then, on 15 May 1944, she received another telegram in which the War Department "established the fact that your son's death occurred on twenty-seven November Nineteen Forty Three." Apparently, a promised letter of explanation from the government never reached

Mrs. Collins. In late 1993, Anita Guidry read a newspaper article marking the fiftieth anniversary of the catastrophe and, upon further investigation, confirmed her suspicion that her brother had indeed been on the *Rohna*.[8] Many other families had similar experiences, never receiving any further word beyond "missing in action."

The Sward family of Linby, Iowa, never found out any particulars about the death of their son, George, on the *Rohna*. "For several years after the war Dad wrote letters trying to find out anything about how George died. However, he either received letters that said no information was available or no answer at all. Finally in hurt and anger he gave up. He died in February 1960, without even knowing the name of the ship George was on."[9]

On 3 January 1944, the War Department wrote to Mrs. Lola A. Nelson in Salt Lake City, Utah, that her husband, Douglas, was missing in action[10] "in the North African Area." However, another letter dated 27 March 1944 informed Mrs. Nelson that her husband had died, adding, "It is regretted that for reasons of military security neither the name of the ship nor other details may be disclosed at this time. The exact location of the disaster cannot be given; however latest reports indicate that it occurred in the European theater and not in the North African area as you were previously advised."[11]

A large, front-page headline in the 18 February 1944 issue of the *New York Times* (the same information was printed by both the Associated Press and United Press) read "1,000 Saved of 2,000 on Ship in Biggest Transport Loss; War Department Gives European Waters as Disaster Scene; Enemy Attack is Attributed to a Submarine." The article began: "One Thousand American soldiers have lost their lives in the sinking of a troopship after an enemy attack in heavy seas in European waters. . . . Details were withheld."[12] It went on to say that U.S. officials gave no indication of just when or where the tragedy occurred. The military report said, "there is a reason to believe that the enemy does not know of the

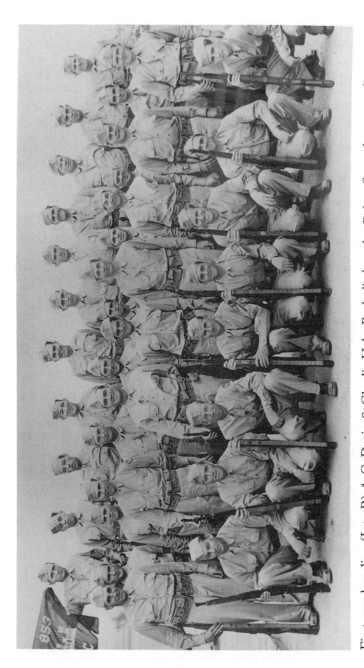

First row, kneeling (L to R): 1. C. Davis; 8. Charlie Hale. Both died on the *Rohna*. Second row, standing (L to R): 4. Livingston Collins; 5. Elmer Ashworth. Both died on the *Rohna*. 10. Sherman Almond. Survived the *Rohna*.

results of this attack and therefore the date is withheld."[13] Obviously, however, the Germans knew they had destroyed a ship on 26 November 1943 in the Mediterranean.

This tragedy of an unknown ship, said the *Times*, "was the worst American wartime disaster of its kind . . . from the point of view of military personnel lost." The *Times* speculated further that since none of the survivors had been landed in British ports, the disaster could have occurred in the Mediterranean. Then the article backtracked a bit, guessing that "it is possible the survivors were landed in Iceland or returned to the Western Hemisphere."[14]

Long after the war ended, both the British and American governments showed a marked reluctance to allow any information on the *Rohna* to leak out. Even today there are many families who lost loved ones on the *Rohna* and still cannot confirm it.[15]

Boards of Inquiry

The first American board of inquiry began its procedures in January 1944 and continued through February. The commanding general of the CBI theater was ordered by the War Department to set up a questionnaire for *Rohna* survivors upon their arrival in India and China. The chief objective of this board was to determine the status of those still missing in action. To be interviewed were the men from the 853rd Engineering Battalion, 322nd Fighter Control Squadron, 31st Signal Construction Battalion, 44th Portable Surgical Hospital, Shipments AD 664 A, 1826 A & D, and RH 705 AAA (all Army Air Force fillers), and Shipment GH 826 (ground fillers). The U.S. government wanted to know the details of the attack, specifically the time of attack, number of German aircraft, number of bombs that hit the ship, where the bombs hit, the force and effect of the explosion, whether fire resulted, and injuries to personnel.[16]

Also, the men were asked when the "abandon ship" order was given and how, whether the ship was abandoned in an "orderly fashion," and about the condition of lifeboats and rafts and "whether all were utilized." They were asked further about visibility out in the water, as well as temperature, force and direction of the wind, and the turbulence of the waves. Were there any rations on board the lifeboats? Did the life preservers work properly? Did the lascar crew help or hinder the evacuation of the *Rohna*. Had there been sufficient boat drills on board the ship? Were any living survivors remaining in the water when you were picked up? Would it have been possible for rescue ships to overlook any living survivors? What was the length of time between the explosion and the sinking of the *Rohna?* Finally, the War Department wanted to know which ship picked up each individual survivor, and to which port they were taken.

War Department officials believed that twenty-five responses to these questions would be sufficient to get an accurate picture of what happened to the *Rohna*. (In all, however, about 100 depositions were taken). Accounts varied about the "abandon ship" order, panic on the decks, the conditions of the sea, and the time the *Rohna* sank. But almost all respondents were consistent in their criticism, even condemnation, of the lascar crew. "The Indian crewmen were inefficient due to their fear for their own safety"; "The Indian crewmen did nothing but try to keep everybody out of the lifeboats which they had taken."[17] Too often, however, due to lack of space on the questionnaires, men were forced to give truncated responses, with "I don't know" given more times than the War Department wanted to hear. Consequently, no conclusive evidence about the *Rohna* was gleaned from these questionnaires.

Continued Efforts to Find Victims

On 1 March 1944 the U.S. Adjutant General's office sent a list of casualties to Gen. Joseph Stilwell, CBI commander, "for the purpose of disposing of mail addressed to personnel" who had been on board the *Rohna*. The adjutant general, Daniel P. Poteet, added, "If any of the personnel listed herein as 'missing in action' have returned to duty under your command, request that you report" their duty status. Sadly, the CBI had nothing new to report.[18]

Well after the war ended and long after it became clear no men listed as "missing in action" would be found miraculously alive, recovery teams continued to work in the Mediterranean and all waters where Americans had suffered casualties, doing everything possible to retrieve their fallen comrades. Time and water, however, made it impossible for them to do so. On 10 September 1948 a report was made to the Quartermaster General in Washington, D.C., that area search and recovery for the Mediterranean Zone was considered "terminated as of 1 September 1948," making it official that 829 GIs from the *Rohna* now were classified as "unrecoverable."[19] It was with a feeling of profound sadness that the Quartermaster General's office declared the case closed. However, all of the paperwork directly concerning the *Rohna* was not completed until 1949. In July the "Final Determination Section" of the Memorial Division's Identification Branch recommended that the previous findings—that 829 of the victims could not be recovered—be accepted.[20] Finally, a meeting of the American Graves Registration Service, Mediterranean Zone, chaired by Maj. Townsend C. Anderson, was convened in Rome on 9 November 1949, and the members accepted all prior recommendations. The paperwork on the *Rohna* had at last been completed.

A few years after the war, a Wall of Missing was erected in the North African American Cemetery in Carthage, Tunisia. Starting with Jacob E. Adamczyk and working its way through to Andrew Zura, the Wall lists 417 members of the 853rd Engineering Aviation Battalion who were lost on the *Rohna* or subsequently at sea. (The British, Australian, and Indian victims were buried in various English military cemeteries in and around Carthage.) As late as 1986, however, the authorities at the Carthage facility did not know the story behind these numbers. The assistant superintendent

Charles Finch in India after the *Rohna* ordeal.

of the cemetery, Joel L. Felz, wondered about the disproportionate numbers of the 853rd listed on the wall. He contacted the superintendent of the British Commonwealth Cemeteries in North Africa and learned that these victims came from a ship named the *Rohna*. Felz could find no mention of the destruction of the *Rohna* in any official histories of the U.S. Army during World War II.[21]

GIs: In the CBI

From Bombay, many *Rohna* survivors rode on another narrow-gauge railroad, this time across an entire country on a trip that took over two weeks. Like the train they rode on the way to Bizerte, this one sometimes went so slowly that the men would get out and walk or jog beside it.[22] Unlike then, however, the weather was hot, and the men were weakened not only by their ordeal on the *Rohna*, but from the inoculations they had been given to protect them from tropical diseases. One of the few interesting moments of this trip occurred when several men ran up to *Rohna* survivor Andy Kalyan's compartment and informed him that they were entering the Indian town of Kalyan. Kalyan has never forgotten "that Indian town having the same name as mine!"[23]

Arriving in Calcutta, the various units went in several different directions. Some men went to Assam, in extreme northern India, while others, like Merker, were sent to the southern city of Bangalore, where they helped to train members of the Royal Indian Air Force and set up communications systems. Some of the *Rohna* survivors were assigned to various U.S. Army Air Forces bombing units in India in the proximity of Burma. One of these survivors was Phythian, who observed with interest that, in mid-1944, U.S. bombers were knocking out bridges in Burma with what he believed to be the same type of bomb that had destroyed the *Rohna*. "They [the bombs] were called the 'bridge-burners.' I can't say how it worked but . . . in 1944 the U.S. had that type of bomb."[24]

The majority of *Rohna* survivors stayed in India and Burma, but a number of them went on to China and served in the Kweilin, Kunming, and Chengtu areas. Portions of the 853rd were there, as well as the 322nd, 44th, and others. A few of the infantrymen wound up in the famed "Merrill's Marauders." Other soldiers joined Clare Chennault's "Flying Tigers" of the 14th Air Force. The main purpose of the men in China, however, was to train Chinese soldiers to fight against the Japanese and build runways for the B-29s of Gen. Curtis LeMay's 21st Bombardment Group.

Zirkle, serving in the Kweilin and Kunming regions, worried not just about the Japanese. Chinese bandits roamed the area, robbing and killing. Also, well before the war ended, a fight was brewing between the French and their colonial charges in Indochina. The Indochinese reported that several guns (which, ironically, had been

Rohna survivors in China.

issued to them by the French) were out of commission, inhibiting their ability to fight the Japanese. Zirkle, who had learned quite a bit of Chinese, was assigned to cross the border of China into Indochina and repair these guns. Once across, he had armed escorts, the leader of which rode a white horse and spoke perfect English. "He was a well-educated man and he hated the French as they just exploited his people, and he hoped that someday they would leave" and allow the Indochinese to live in peace.[25] The man's name, according to Zirkle, was Ho Chi Minh.

By the summer and early fall of 1945, the *Rohna* survivors were poised, along with thousands of other GIs, to invade the Japanese homeland itself. The atomic bombings of Hiroshima and Nagasaki spared them from making such a move, and they cheered loudly

Aaron Weber in China along the Burma Road.

Some *Rohna* survivors in China. Front row: Howard A. Devlin, John P. Fievet, Vincent J. Fonte, John Slujinsky; back row: Richard E. Earhart, Eugene C. Breedlove, Pascual Castro, C. Bradley, Robert L. Sherrill.

when the Japanese surrendered. Their thoughts now turned to home and how they would get there. Most of the officers flew back (since they had priority over the enlisted), while the majority of enlisted men came back on troop transports such as the *Marine Robin,* heading for San Francisco or Seattle. One enlisted man, Phythian, noted that his outfit was flying bombers back to their U.S. bases—why, therefore, shouldn't he be on one of them? "I didn't care to come home on a ship. *Thanks but no thanks!*"[26] Arthur Meyer returned on the *Elotyn,* a ship that was known as the "Queen of the Pacific"—in 1913. [27]

Eugene Piquard, who had not been on the *Rohna,* but had met many of her survivors in China, returned home to Illinois in November 1945 by way of the Mediterranean. His ship, the *Callan,* retraced the path that many of his buddies in the 31st had taken two years before on the *Rohna.* "As the *Callan* safely steamed by the location of the *Rohna* disaster, a memorial service was held on the fantail of the ship." All smoking and recreational activities were ordered stopped during this service. Lt. H. Braun, a *Rohna* survivor (who had offered his life belt to Walter Randis) retold the circumstances of the sinking, and all on board, including many of the survivors, "solemnly remembered their comrades who had been lost. The Captain said a brief prayer and then a squad of marines fired a rifle salute." Taps was played, and the *Callan* continued homeward.[28]

"Homeward." It was a precious word to these young men. Obviously they were not the same men who had left three or four years earlier. Their experiences had changed their perspectives on the world and on life itself. "We have done our share in winning the war," the chronicler of the 853rd said, "so that we might have the opportunity to build a meaningful future. . . . We will go back with a better understanding of the world and its peoples." And then, perhaps, the most important lesson: "We have learned to appreciate deeply so much we took for granted before, both the little comforts of living, and those persons whom we love; in fact, everything that is symbolized by that magic word, HOME!"[29] Someone drew a picture of a young, helmeted, rifle-bearing soldier standing by a gravestone. The caption read: "Tell Them When You Go Home, For Their Tomorrows We Gave Our Today."

Guilt Feelings

Most of the *Rohna* survivors were discharged in 1945, but their traumas did not go away; if anything, they worsened. The men either resumed their old lives upon returning or went into new fields altogether. Though they readjusted fairly well to civilian society, for the next fifty years many asked themselves, "Why me?" "Why was I saved in the tragedy and my good buddy was not?" Soldiers become close to each other, especially during a war. There is a bond that transcends religious, ethnic, and regional differences; they think of themselves as one. The guilt surfaced for the survivors of the *Rohna* because they felt that, by surviving, they had betrayed their fallen comrades. One author has written, "Sometimes veterans won't recognize it [survival guilt] as self-punishment, thinking that by not forgiving themselves they somehow honor all the losses experienced. To forgive oneself, and others, might mean putting some of [the survivor guilt] behind, and this in a sense creates further guilt, resulting in a self-perpetuating cycle—one that traps the veteran in a desert of grief."[30]

Over the years Hunter, who lives in Maine, has kept in touch with Finch, in Texas. "We both find that at times we get a guilt feeling and maybe a little misty eyed when we think of all our good friends who had to die. Why them and not us?"[31] Smith has been trying to "forget the personal horror" for fifty years. "Why relive the tragedy and punish one's self with so much emotional stress?"[32]

But it was not just the *Rohna* survivors who suffered from guilt over the next several years. If anything, those on board the *Karoa*, *Banfora*, as well as several other ships in the convoy, felt the same way, since they had seen the *Rohna* victims out in the water but were under orders not to stop for them. Thomas Hooks, on the *Karoa*, "felt guilty for quite a while that we did not turn back to rescue many men overboard, swimming and on rafts. . . . It was a sad and frustrating sight—always vivid in my mind."[33]

Adding to this profound sense of guilt, some of the survivors also suffered from flashbacks, anxiety attacks, and disillusionment about the postwar years. Many remained relatively quiet about it through the years, revealing their feelings only decades later. A recent study indicates that with the fiftieth anniversary of the end of World War II, "many vets have visited Veterans Affairs hospitals with complaints of sleeplessness, nightmares, flashbacks, crying spells, and other symptoms."[34] Some of these complaints were "painfully emotional, about experiences they haven't told a soul about."[35] It was retirement from their work or careers that caused these vets to think about their experiences in World War II. The generation of World War II, said one psychologist, has lived their lives in the "John Wayne" image; but later on they paid a price "because it's so hard to hold back human emotions at that level."[36]

For one survivor, post-*Rohna* life held a great irony. Quick, and his best friend and fellow survivor, Vernie L. Thomas, had received their Purple Hearts together, and after the war the two regularly corresponded. Then Quick didn't hear from Thomas for eighteen months. Concerned, Quick wrote to inquire if anything was wrong. Thomas's sister wrote back that Tommy had died—he had drowned while bass fishing on a lake near his home. "Just didn't make sense to me for a long time," Quick reflected.[37]

But despite the problems of readjusting to civilian life in 1945, the majority of the *Rohna* survivors overcame their traumas, held steady jobs over the next half century, and provided admirably for their families. A few of the survivors stayed in touch with one another, and some tried to get information, governmental or otherwise, on the sinking of the *Rohna*. Each effort was met by a wall of bureaucratic refusals. Around 1960 Colonel Virden thought about writing on the tragedy. Since he was still in the army, he had to obtain Pentagon permission to do so. But he was refused on the grounds that any writing on the subject might possibly be embarrassing to the British government. Virden's book was never written.[38]

"Fifty Years of Life"

The first reunion ever of the *Rohna* survivors—which included many veterans of the *Pioneer, Banfora, Egra, Karoa,* and *Rajula*—was held in 1993 in Gatlinburg, Tennessee. Many had to bring snapshots with them to show others what they looked like in 1943–1945. "Some of us walked slowly, used canes and wanted to sit down right away. We had to bridge that fifty year gap."[39] As survivor Andrew Fetsko described, "it took some speaking to each other before our personalities hit a right chord, and something we said or did would make us recall" each others' names. After recognizing each other, the men went on to have joyful, sometimes tearful, reunions. Often a *Rohna* man, during a speech, would thank the *Pioneer* crew (including the skipper, "Roy" Rogers) in attendance for "giving me an additional fifty years of life."

Epilogue

After the fateful day of 26 November 1943, Major Dochtermann flew several additional missions. He was in eastern Germany in 1945 when he was taken as prisoner of war. He was held in England, at Stratford-upon-Avon, in a camp especially built for high-ranking German officers. He was released on 10 May 1946 and immediately returned to Germany, where he quickly readjusted to civilian life. About his role on 26 November 1943, he said, "I was a front line soldier." He had taken the oath of service, and he had to follow orders. Today, he "damns every war," and "the memory of all

the fallen soldiers, from whichever nation, makes me deeply sad."[40]
For him, Dochtermann said in an interview, "the war will end only
on the day I die." As for the *Rohna* survivors, he has said of them:
"I give them my sincere greetings, everyone of them."[41]

On Veterans Day 1993, Borows listened to the radio while driving his car to a garage for some repairs. Charles Osgood came on,
and his program that day was about HMT *Rohna*, and her destruction a half century ago. Borows listened in disbelief. He and many
of his long-lost comrades around the country had not heard through
the growing *Rohna* "network" that Osgood was to include them in
his program. "I had to pull off the road," Borows said. "I couldn't
believe it!"[42]

Osgood noted the USS *Arizona* and her horrible destruction.
But her fate has gone into many history books written about World
War II. The new kind of German bomb that destroyed the *Rohna*,
he said, accounted for the cloak of secrecy and the Allies' reticence
to publicize it. But her victims were just as real and as tragic as
those found in any other sinking or great battle in World War II.
"It just doesn't seem right," Osgood remarked, "that so many
should have died in the sinking of the *Rohna* and that so few people" have remembered.[43]

But Osgood summed up everything with his closing sentence:
"It's not that we forgot. It's that we never knew."

Appendix A

Rohna Poems

Louis J. DiFolco, "The Pioneer Comes Through."
Sung to the tune of "Casey Jones."

Now fill up your glasses folks, and turn off the jazz,
  Everybody lend me all the ears he has.
I'm going to tell a story dealt with fame and fear,
  About the A.M. sweeper called the Pioneer.

Now the mighty "Rohna" was in the race,
  and to the name they gave her—she was no disgrace.
First a cloud of smoke, and then the flame,
  But she'll always be remembered as a ship of fame.

Now I've heard them moan, and I've heard them cry,
  I never knew disaster till I saw some die.
Now some were burnt and some were froze,
  Others fell off the cargo nets in eternal doze.

Now the fight was over—the results were fair,
    Twelve Nazi bombers were forced out of the air.
Now with the help of God, and the angels too,
    The mighty baby escort Pioneer pulled through.

CHORUS
Now the Pioneer was fighting for our colors
    Fighting for the Land we love to roam
We'll fight right on—until we hear the whistle,
    Then we'll lash our hammocks, and we'll all go home.

Harrell Jones, untitled

She was an angel of the sea
    She did not stand by her grave and weep
She was not there, she did not sleep
    She was a fighter of the deep.
She fought for country and flag to keep
    She was a thousand winds that blow
She fought like a diamond bent on snow
    She was like the sunlight on ripened grain
She was like the gentle Autumn rain.
    She cut through the sea at night
Like the birds in circling flight
    She was the water caressing the shore
She rode the waves as never before
    She did not stand by her grave and cry
She was not there; she did not die
    She was the Angel of the Sea, for it was meant to be.

Anonymous

We had no thought of fear that day,
Our spirits soaring high;
And we never dreamed that danger lurked
In that calm and peaceful sky.

On the 26th at 4:30 p.m.
The Jerries came in fast,
A destroyer sped across our bow
And gave the planes a blast.

Our guns were blazing all around;
Their shots were not in vain,
A Nazi plane went down in smoke
Another burst in flame.

The ack-ack guns were roaring now;
The sky was black with smoke,
The Nazis took a turn about
And soon all hell broke out.

The order came to go below,
We were not a happy bunch,
It was as if we seemed to know
Or perhaps we had a hunch.

There were no hysterics of fear at all,
At least it didn't show.
Some played cards, others smoked
While they waited for the blow.

It was dark and hot down in the hold,
We had no chance to fight.
Would we have a chance if the ship were hit?
We hoped and prayed we might.

The bombs were falling all around,
*   Our guns kept up a steady roar.*
They missed us time and time again,
*   But still came back with more.*

Every time a bomb fell close
*   Our ship would rock and shake.*
Our gunners gave them all they had,
*   There were so many lives at stake.*

Suddenly the ship was hit,
*   She shuddered from stern to stem.*
The lights went out, the engines stopped
*   And would never go again.*

Shrapnel flew and men were hit
*   And timber fell like rain,*
The Rohna gave out a burst of smoke
*   And then burst into flame.*

The order came from up above
*   For all to come on deck,*
And that we did without a shove
*   And gazed upon the wreck.*

There seemed to be no panic,
*   We kept pretty level heads,*
Though many of the boys were hurt
*   And many of them dead.*

Some of the boys were trapped below
*   In the hatch where the missile fell.*
What they went through we will never know
*   For none of them lived to tell.*

We tried to lower boats and rafts
　　But all to no avail,
All we got was the small ones
　　Which we were throwing over the rail.

The water was rough and black with men
　　In the quickly failing light.
We were fighting death with all we had
　　And praying with all our might.

For two and one half hours
　　The Jerries gave us hell,
But our thoughts were on surviving
　　The rough and angry swells.

We swam on and on as best we could
　　A minesweeper was our goal.
We knew we had no time to lose
　　For the sea was taking its toll.

The screams of men was sickening;
　　They sent chills up and down our spine.
We knew they were coming from buddies of ours
　　Friends of yours and mine.

The Nazis came back for a final attack
　　Determined, we were to lose.
Many a man was cut to death
　　As he was sucked into the screw.

Night set in and was inky black
　　The water was freezing cold.
We prayed for a ship to take us back
　　And a blanket in which to roll.

In the distance the Rohna gave a final shudder
    She fought and she was brave
Until the moment she disappeared
    Into her watery grave.
We lost a lot of men that day,
    One third of us remain;
But we know the men who died that way
    Have not done so in vain.
We think of those buddies
    Wherever they may be,
And we will never forget the battle
    of Men against the sea.

Anonymous

It was on a Friday evening
    Just about five o'clock
When the great "Rohna"
    Began to reel and rock.

The fellows they all cry
    What shall we do
The ship has been hit
    And we can't go through.

Our ship was sinking rapidly
    And going mighty fast
We had to leave her quickly
    They knew it couldn't last.

The sea was really angry
    And the waves, they were too
But God was there with us
    And he saw us through.

Now we are on our way again
  And all getting well
To go through that again, Boys
  Would certainly be hell.

Anonymous

It was on a Friday evening in Nov.
  And the wind was very high,
When we got the report
  There were German planes up in the sky.

Now when they attacked
  They came in on the sun
But they soon found out
  We had a man on every gun.

But our ship was numbered
  And the Nazis found their mark
The great ship "Rohna" went down
  Just after dark.

Now the water was full of men
  And they were all my buddies too
But I know that God is taking care
  of those that didn't pull through.

Appendix B

Where Are They Now?

Upon his return to Alabama, Fievet got a degree under the GI Bill at Birmingham-Southern College and worked for forty-five years as a buyer and purchasing consultant for United States Steel in Birmingham. His Alabama pal, Childress, also went to college, majoring in animal science, but spent his career as the owner of a retail shoe store. "I'll describe myself," he said in 1994, "as a family man, and one who gives thanks to my Heavenly Father daily for life itself."

Finch, from Los Fresnos, Texas, became a freelance writer, specializing in fishing, railroads, and history. Hollimon earned a B.A. degree from Mississippi Southern University and an M.A. from Louisiana State University, and spent thirty-five years as a teacher, coach, principal, and superintendent in the Louisiana school system. Peach became a bus driver, but wound up as a postal employee until his retirement in 1981. Smith became a banker, rising to the position of senior vice president of a statewide system in Virginia.

Muchnick spent his career as a broker and insurance agent with his own company. Mason became an automobile mechanic, owning his own business. Then, he "saw the writing on the wall," and sold his company to two of his employees, and began a job with International Business Machines, which he kept until his retirement in the 1980s. Brewer rose to the rank of colonel before his retirement from the Air Force in 1965. After that he worked for a computerized credit reporting network for fifteen years. Then he "retired to his yard, and some golf." For the D-Day commemorations in 1994, he was chosen by the Air Communications Services to deliver a plaque to French officials in Normandy.

While in India, Caskey went to a USO show one night. There he met Maddie Zoulal, a singer and dancer in a show, "Happy Holliday." In 1995, they celebrated their 48th wedding anniversary. Caskey had been a student at Findlay College in Ohio before the war and worked for an import-export firm for many years after returning to civilian life. As soon as Inks got home, he married his high school sweetheart and resumed work as a recapper for a small tire company. After a time he bought the company and ran it for thirty years before his retirement. After his discharge, Kroog, who had worked in a delicatessen before the war, worked for seventeen years as a repairman and handyman for a propane company. Then he went back into the deli business with his brother. Granfield took a civil service test and became a police officer in Springfield, Massachusetts, a position he held for thirty years. Horton became a petroleum geologist, working for twenty-eight years with other companies before forming his own in 1986. Gibson practiced law in Dillon, South Carolina, for many years. Ashley worked with Bell Aircraft and Bendix Aviation. Miles became a meat cutter for the Safeway supermarket chain. Dana went back to his old job in a papermill. Edwards worked many years for the C & O Railroad. And Zirkle became a photographer.

Columbus, Ohio: *Rohna*/KMF-26 Reunion, 5–7 May 1995

Standing at an exhibit table, *Pioneer* crew member Ernest Croyle looked up to see *Rohna* survivor Ernest Horton beside him. The two men stared intently at one another for about a minute before simultaneously recognizing each other. Horton quietly said to Croyle: "You're the one who pulled me out of the water." Their handshake turned into an embrace; the two men had not seen or heard of one another for the past fifty-two years, since the night of 26 November 1943.

The closeness that began on that night was resurrected here in Columbus, Ohio, at the second reunion of the *Rohna* and *Pioneer* and personnel from other ships, such as the *Egra, Karoa, Banfora,* and *Rajula.* Harrell Jones, or "Jonesy," the "red-headed sailor" who saved so many men, was there; so was his shipmate, Bellomy, who proudly told everyone that he is from West "by God" Virginia; and Fievet, who did so much over the years to make the story of the *Rohna* publicly known, was there, along with dozens of other comrades.

Many of these men still spoke in the present tense when recounting their experiences of being shot out of the sea. "Reed knows better than to go to the latrine looking for a porthole when we're under attack," Schoenacker said. "He should be out here on the deck, ready to go overboard." Out in the hallway, Lacy, from the *Rohna,* scoffs at the *Pioneer*'s David Lewis, telling him, "Your ship didn't stop for me the first time. Went right on by me." Lewis rejoins, "Didn't stop because you didn't have the right politics. Still don't."

Of course, there was much good-natured bantering and jovialty. One *Pioneer* man told a *Rohna* man that ever since that night his hands had been "un-matched; one was right and the other left," he explained. And, of course, one corny joke always led to another. Since most of the *Rohna* men had gone on to China, Burma, and

India, one of them at the reunion asked if everybody understood what CBI meant. Yes, came the answer: The letters referred to the China-Burma-India theater of war. No, came the rejoinder: They stood for "Confused Beyond Imagination."

When it came time for the photo shoot, master of ceremonies Canney asked that the men follow their respective officers or sergeants out to the foyer. Ron Wright, from the *Pioneer*, called out, "All right men, follow me!" And they did. As they sat to be photographed, with a large number of *Rohna* survivors looking on, the *Pioneer* veterans would not be still for the photographer and cut up so much that a *Rohna* man quipped, "Are these really the people who rescued us?"

Indeed they were, and the passing of half a century has not dimmed their memories, or the pride they feel in having been caught up in a historical event. They, with their *Rohna* brothers, still feel neglected by the U.S. and British governments. *Why* do they not even today have the recognition they feel they deserve? Certainly, they stand in respectful memory of the USS *Arizona* and the USS *Indianapolis;* they wish neither had happened any more than they would have willed the destruction of the *Rohna*. But as Charles Osgood said, the *Arizona* and the *Indianapolis* have always received full press; the *Rohna* received very little, if any.

Such sentiments do not mean the *Rohna* survivors or any of their rescuers feel bitter toward the U.S. and British governments; perplexed, yes, but bitter, no. One would not find a more patriotic group of individuals who dearly love their country than the survivors of the *Rohna*, the rescuers from the *Pioneer*, and the other Americans in KMF-26. Many of those at the reunion stood before the microphone on the Clarion Hotel plaza and gave personal descriptions of their ordeal and testimony to the allegiance they possess for their country.

Also speaking at the reunion were two NOKs (next of kin). James Blaine of California lovingly remembered his lost brother,

Frank, while James Bennett of Clinton, Washington, told the group that he had always wondered what his brother, Robert, would have been like in his older years. Seeing Robert's comrades now, he knew, and was pleased.

After the banquet on Saturday night, the Song Spinners of Westerville, Ohio, sang patriotic songs, which was followed by a sing-along led by Maddie Caskey. Songs such as "White Cliffs of Dover," "A Nightingale Sang on Berkeley Square," "Remember Pearl Harbor," "As Time Goes By," "Sentimental Journey," and several others brought tears to the eyes of more than one of those in attendance. And, at the urging of her husband Bill and to the thorough delight of her audience, Maddie closed the show with a stirring a cappella rendition of "Summertime."

During the memorial services, host Canney called for a moment of silence to remember those who were lost on the *Rohna*, as well as for those *Rohna* men who had died since the end of the war in 1945.

And what of the future regarding more *Rohna* reunions? Some say they can't wait for the next one. Others feel that perhaps it is time to give them up. After all, they argue, the overwhelming majority of *Rohna* survivors are in their seventies, some in their eighties, so perhaps they should put the past—collectively, at least; they would never be able to do so on a personal basis—behind them.

As the reunion drew to a close, many men didn't really want to leave. They wanted to linger, say just one more thing to their comrades. Reluctantly, though, they boarded the airport shuttles, got into their cars, and waved a cheerful good-bye to everyone in sight. Even if there are no more reunions, the love and closeness that these men have for one another most assuredly will be everlasting.

Notes

Chapter 1: A Thanksgiving to Remember

1. Eugene C. Breedlove, "Sinking of H.M.T. Rohna, November 26, 1943," unpublished essay, n.d.; Breedlove, letter to the author, 22 January 1994.
2. Ulys Jackson, "My World War Two Memoirs," in Mrs. Ulys Jackson, *David and Anney (Bowen) Jackson in Tennessee and Arkansas: Some Ancestors and Descendants* (Point Lookout, Missouri: The School of the Ozarks Press, 1977), 28.
3. Robert Brewer, "The Sinking of the Rohna," interview by Larry Morrison, 4 October 1984, U.S. Air Force Albert F. Simpson Historical Research Center, Scott Air Force Base, Illinois.
4. Tom Suchan, "Voyage of Death," *Beacon-Journal* (Akron, Ohio), 18 November 1973, 6.
5. William Quick, letter to the author, 24 June 1994.
6. British War Diary Monthly Summary, November 1943, Admiralty Files, Public Records Office (PRO), Kew, London.
7. Ibid.
8. James L. Shaw, "Rajula—A Liner Unsung but not Forgotten," *Ships Monthly* (June 1980): 27.
9. Report, Commodore Wakeman-Coleville, December 1943, Admiralty File 199, PRO.

10. Suchan, "Voyage," 6.
11. Ibid., 7–8.
12. Charles Finch, "The Rohna: Why The Secret?" Unpublished, undated essay. One official U.S. government report from the War Department (AG 704 DEAD, 5 May 1944) put the number of American passengers aboard the Rohna at 1,981. Apparently the British government never reported on this matter. Invariably over the years, there have been differences between *Rohna* survivors and government statistics. "I have an awful inner feeling that there were many more aboard the *Rohna* than the ones they [various governmental agencies] listed. I have at hand, two listings from survivors totalling well over 150 men—and none are listed anywhere in any of the records we have. . . . Also—I have never read any reports of my own five buddies. . . . Why aren't these listed?" William Caskey, letter to the author, undated, 1994.
13. See Carlton Jackson, A Social History of the Scotch-Irish (Lanham, Maryland: Madison Press, 1993).
14. John Fievet, "World War II's Secret Disaster," *American History* 29(3) (August 1994): 27.
15. John Harding, letter to the author, 9 March 1995; Harding diary, unpublished, 25 March 1943.
16. Wallace Mason, letter to the author, 31 August 1994.
17. James Loper, letter to the author, 31 December 1994.
18. Don Fortune, "It's Time—after 50 Years—to recognize the sinking of the Rohna," *San Francisco Examiner,* 25 July 1993.
19. John L. Smith, "Memories Recalled Fifty Years After the HMT Rohna Disaster on November 26, 1943," unpublished essay, 1993.
20. Ibid.
21. James Pope interview (telephone), January 1995.
22. Keith Eubank, *Summit at Tehran* (New York: William Morrow and Company, 1985), 167.
23. Paul D. Mayle, *Eureka Summit: Agreement in Principle and the Big Three at Teheran, 1943* (Newark, Delaware: University of Delaware Press, 1987), 49.
24. John Harding, letter to the author, 7 March 1995.
25. Master of *Reina del Pacifico* to Commodore Wakeman-Colville aboard the *Ranchi,* 2 December 1943, Admiralty 199, PRO.
26. H. Pickering, letter to the author, 8 March 1995.
27. Carl Schoenacker diary; Schoenacker letter to the author, 20 June 1994.
28. This account of the 853rd comes from its unit history, "The 853rd Engineer Aviation Battalion," undated, unpublished.
29. Ibid., 6.
30. John Fievet, "The H.M.T. Rohna: The Untold Story," unpublished manuscript, 11 November 1993.

31. Simon Muchnick, letter to the author, 23 May 1994; H. C. B. Rogers, *Troopships and their History* (London: Seeley Services, 1963), 195.
32. Schoenacker letter.
33. John Smith, letter to the author, 30 October 1994; Smith, "Memories."
34. Ernest H. Horton, "Excerpts From the Diary," undated; Horton, letter to the author, 6 May 1994.
35. Hank Kuberski, "World War II's Best Kept Secret: The Sinking of the HMT *Rohna,* November 26, 1943; With the Loss of 1015 Men; The British Convoy, KMF 26, undated, unpublished essay, 1.
36. Admiralty War Diary; Summary, November 1943, PRO.
37. Breedlove letter; Breedlove, "Sinking of H.M.T. Rohna."
38. Ibid.
39. Ibid.
40. Loper letter.
41. Horton, "Diary," 1.
42. Thomas Conway, letter to the author, 28 November 1994.
43. Milton Garret, letter to the author, 4 March 1995.
44. J. Don Sullivan, letter to the author, 7 March 1995.
45. Loper letter.
46. Hilary St. George Saunders, *Valiant Voyaging: A Short History of the British India Steam Navigation Company in the Second World War 1939–1945* (London: Faber and Faber Ltd.), 87.
47. Conway letter, 28 November 1994.
48. HMS *Zamalak* Report, 1942, Admiralty 199, PRO.
49. James Blaine, letter to the author, 1 March 1995; Barbara O'Haver, letter to the author, 2 March 1995.
50. Rogers, *Troopships,* 195.
51. Fortune, "It's Time," A-1; Raymond J. Boylan, M.D., letter to the author, 18 May 1994; James Lacy, letter to the author, n.d., 1994. Smith, "Memories," 4.
52. Camdon Inks, letter to the author, 23 May 1994.
53. Loper letter.
54. Suchan, "Voyage," 5–8.
55. Jasper Spain, letter to the author, 13 March 1995.

Chapter 2: Attack!

1. Hans Dochtermann, "Angriff Auf Den U S Geleitzug KMF 26 Vor Der Bucht Von Bougie," (Frankfurt, Germany, 14 July 1992), unpublished essay, 1.

2. Hans Dochtermann, letter to the author, 4 October 1994.
3. Dochtermann, "Angriff," 2.
4. Tom Huntington, "V-2, The Long Shadow," *Air and Space* (February/March 1993), 81.
5. J. R. Smith and Anthony L. Kay, *German Aircraft of the Second World War* (Baltimore, Maryland: The Nautical & Aviation Publishing Company of America, 1972), 676–677.
6. Ibid.
7. Ibid.
8. Smith and Kay, *German Aircraft*, 677.
9. A discussion of "Azon" and "Razon" is found in John Quick, *Dictionary of Weapons and Military Terms* (New York: McGraw-Hill, 1973), 42.
10. William McCullough, recorded tape sent to the author, March 1995.
11. Dr. Lothar Weiss, letter to the author, 3 August 1994.
12. Dochtermann, "Angriff," 5.
13. Ibid.
14. Ibid.
15. Ibid, 7–10.
16. Ibid.
17. Forrest Diehl, tape to the author, n.d., 1994; Wilmot Boone, M.D., letter to the author, 20 January 1994.
18. Ibid.
19. Fievet, "The Untold Story," 4.
20. J. B. Gibson, letter to the author, 16 May 1994.
21. Charles Finch, "The Rohna," unpublished essay, n.d., 3; Charles Finch, letter to the author, 24 January 1994.
22. Thomas Randall, letter to the author, 14 March 1995.
23. USS *Pioneer* Action Report, 26 November 1943, Washington, D.C, The National Archives.
24. Diehl tape; Boone letter.
25. John J. Donovan to Senator Irving Ives, 28 December 1950. In the papers of Carl Schoenacker.
26. Interviews with Lt. Col. John Frolich and Maj. James Kilpatrick, December 1943, Admiralty, PRO.
27. Thomas J. Hooks, "The Rohna Story," *Ex-CBI Roundup* (July 1986): 6–10. Also in reference to the makeup and operation of the Henschel 293, see Heinz J. Nowarra, *Die Deutsche Luftrustung 1933–1944*, vol. 4 (Koblenz: Bernard & Graefe Verlag, 1993), 66–67; Michael J. Neufeld, *The Rocket and the Reich: Peenemunde and the Coming of the Ballistic Missile Era* (New York: Free Press, 1995), 235.
28. Smith and Kay, *German Aircraft*, 674–77.

29. Dochtermann, "Angriff," 8.
30. Finch, "The Rohna."
31. Charles Clancy, letter to the author, 15 March 1994.
32. Meyer Bronstein, "Report and Critique on Sinking of the HMT *Rohna*," to Chief of Transportation, Department of the Army, Washington, D.C., 17 May 1949, 2.
33. John Rosseau, letter to the author, 23 February 1995.
34. Dan B. McCarthy, "The Fiery Birth of Missile Warfare," *V.F.W. Magazine* 21 (November 1967): 21. Suchan, "Voyage," 8.
35. *Derrick,* 24 November 1993; Bruno Birsa, letter to the author, n.d., 1994.
36. A. M. Kadis, letter to the author, 25 January 1994.
37. Caskey letter; Breedlove, "Sinking of H.M.T. Rohna"; Richard Phythian, Edward Ashley, William Matthews, Russell Cherry, letters to the author, 5 May 1994, 26 April 1994, 24 May 1994, and 30 May 1994; James G. Clounts to J. M. Buckler, 6 August 1987, Clounts collection, Douglasville, Georgia.
38. William F. Wolfe, letter to the author, 8 March 1994.
39. David L. Moak, "One Man Has Never Forgotten," *Herald-Dispatch* (West Virginia), 26 November 1993; Charles Edwards, letter to the author, n.d., 1994.
40. Horton, "Diary."
41. Fred Dettman, letter to the author, n.d., 1994.
42. Robert Loren Van Ausdall, letter to the author, 3 March 1995.
43. Ibid.
44. LeRoy E. Rogers, letter to the author, 23 September 1994; USS *Pioneer* Report, 2 December 1943 (A16-3\F41-G), National Archives. On 26 November 1943, however, a report from the *Pioneer* stated that "the convoy apparently continued on course during attack but speed and zig-zagging plan were not observed" (*Pioneer* Action Report, 26 November 1943). It may well have been that only some of the ships in the convoy failed to execute the zig-zagging patterns, because their speed caused them to lag behind. A War Diary report from HMT *Birmingham* (which had been the flagship of KMF-26 through the Atlantic) dated 25 November 1943 spoke of the "little protection" that could be given to the slower-moving ships (that is, ten knots as opposed to thirteen) (Report, HMT *Birmingham,* 25 November 1943, Admiralty Files, PRO).
45. Hans Dochtermann interview (telephone), 12 January 1995.
46. Extract from "Report of an Interview with the Second Officer of S.S. *Rohna,*" n.d., 1943, AG File, National Archives. See also Hooks, "The Rohna Story," 6.
47. Jasper Spain, letter to the author, 13 March 1995.

48. Inks letter.
49. Dana Hunter, letter to the author, 3 May 1994.
50. R. G. Hand interview (telephone), 8 February 1995.
51. Phythian and Boone letters.
52. Horton, "Diary."
53. Gibson letter.
54. Quick letter.
55. C. Albertus Hewitt, "A Troopship Sinks," *Gateway* (Autumn 1944): 5.
56. Finch, "The Rohna."
57. Rear Adm. Allan Poland to commander-in-chief of the *Levant*, 9 December 1943, Admiralty, PRO. In this same letter, Admiral Poland spoke about the inadequacy of air cover for KMF-26 as she plied eastward through the Mediterranean.
58. HMS *Atherstone* Report, 30 November 1943, Admiralty 199, PRO.
59. T. John Fugill, letter to the author, 12 March 1995.
60. Harrell Jones, letter to the author, n.d., 1994.
61. McCullough tape.
62. Dochtermann, "Angriff," 7–8.
63. Ibid., 8–10.
64. James Rourke, letter to the author, 16 March 1995.
65. Dochtermann, "Angriff," 8–12.
66. Sam Cunigan interview, 20 November 1994, Auburn, Kentucky.
67. Report, 27 November 1943, File Air 27, PRO.
68. Ibid.
69. McCullough tape.
70. William Green, *War Planes of the Third Reich* (New York: Galahad Books, 1967), 345.
71. HMS *Colombo* Report, 27 November 1943, Admiralty, PRO.
72. Spain letter.
73. Dochtermann, "Angriff," 10–15.
74. Ibid, 10.

Chapter 3: The Guided Bomb

1. Dochtermann, "Angriff," 3–11.
2. Ibid.
3. Ibid., 2–13.
4. *Guided Bomb*, TV documentary (New York: Video Ordnance, 1993).
5. Dochtermann, "Angriff," 7–10.
6. Ibid., 8.

7. Ibid.

8. Ibid, 5–12.

9. Ibid.

10. *Guided Bomb.*

11. Ibid.

12. Paul Different, letter to the author, 14 May 1994.

13. McCullough tape.

14. Wrnt. Ofc. Pilot F. B. Forge, "Intelligence Report," 10 December 1943, AG Files, National Archives.

15. War Report, HMS *Miaoules* to commander-in-chief of the *Levant,* 15 December 1943, Admiralty, PRO.

16. Suchan, "Voyage," 5.

17. Hunter letter.

18. Howard Lachtman, "Secret," *Stockton Record,* 22 July 1993.

19. Fievet, "The Untold Story," 6.

20. Suchan, "Voyage," 6.

21. Meredith Barkley, "Big Secret: 50 Years after disaster mystery still surrounds bombing of HMS Rohna," *Ledger* (Eden, North Carolina), 17 October 1993; Cunigan interview.

22. HMS *Arundel Castle* Report, December 1943, Admiralty, PRO.

23. Schoenacker letter.

24. Inks letter.

25. Clarence J. Bailey, letter to the author, n.d., 1994.

26. Kadis letter.

27. McCullough tape.

28. LeRoy Rogers, letter to the author, 22 June 1994.

29. Breedlove, "Missing" 1–6.

30. Moak, "One Man."

31. Loper letter.

32. Schoenacker letter.

33. Hooks, "The Rohna Story," 7.

34. Louis Rees, letter to the author, n.d. , March 1995.

35. Schoenacker letter.

36. William Gordon, "Thankful Survivor," *Newark Star Ledger,* 24 November 1993.

37. Richard Peach, letter to the author, 16 March 1994.

38. Ibid.

39. Schoenacker letter.

40. Robert Brewer, "The Sinking of the Rohna," unpublished essay, 3. From the Brewer collection, Stockton, California.

41. Finch, "The Rohna," 4.

42. M. J. Granfield, letter to the author, 24 January 1994.
43. Finch, "The Rohna."
44. Boone letter.
45. Will Workman, "Every Soldier Has a Story," *Record* (Rock Hill, NY), 21 November 1993.
46. Rosseau letter.
47. George Cardwell, letter to the editor, 9 March 1995.
48. McCullough tape.
49. Suchan, "Voyage," 6–8; Herman Rice, letter to the author, 11 March 1995.
50. Raymond Epifano, letter to the author, n.d., 1994.
51. Hunter letter.
52. Hewitt, "Troopship," 5–6.
53. Ibid.
54. Smith, "Memories," 5–6.
55. 853rd unit history, 1–10.
56. Ibid.
57. Theodore Kroog, letter to the author, 9 March 1994.
58. John Walters, letter to the author, 3 March 1995.
59. Francis Taylor, letter to the author, 9 March 1995.
60. Carl Molesworth, *Wing to Wing: Air Combat in China, 1943–1945* (New York: Orion Books, 1990), 33.
61. Peach letter.
62. Brewer, "Sinking," 4.
63. Peach letter.
64. Ibid.

Chapter 4: Over the Railings

1. Brewer, "Sinking," 3–5.
2. Inks letter.
3. Kroog letter.
4. Epifano letter.
5. Most of the testaments and letters bring up the question of whether any distinct orders were given to abandon ship. The overwhelming majority of responses indicate that the command to abandon the *Rohna* was first given by Captain Murphy to Major Frolich, who then passed it along by word of mouth, because all communications systems had been destroyed.
6. W. L. Butcher Report, 27 November 1943, Admiralty, PRO.
7. Forrest "Bill" Wheeler, letter to the author, 25 May 1994.
8. Finch, "The Rohna," 3.

9. Fievet, "The Untold Story," 7.
10. Parker Childress, letter to the author, 19 January 1994.
11. Herald Miles, letter to the author, 18 May 1994. See also Jane Feller, "Surviving Shipmates Plan 50-year Reunion," *Lassen County Times* (Susanville, California), 3 August 1993.
12. Diehl tape.
13. Mason letter.
14. John P. Canney, letter to the author, 24 March 1994.
15. Smith letter.
16. Bronstein, "Report and Critique."
17. Finch, "The Rohna," 8.
18. Fievet, "Secret Disaster," 30.
19. Phythian letter.
20. Bill McKee, letter to the author, n.d., 1994.
21. Peach letter.
22. Bronstein, "Report and Critique," 2.
23. Horton, "Diary," 8.
24. Buckler letter.
25. Walter D. Zielenski, Statement on the Sinking of the *Rohna*, 5 May 1944, AG 704 DEAD, National Archives.
26. Quick letter.
27. Richard Ferguson, letter to the author, 14 May 1994.
28. Finch, "The Rohna," 5.
29. Canney letter.
30. AG 704 DEAD, 5 May 1944, National Archives.
31. Taylor letter.
32. Finch to Don Fortune, 19 July 1994; Finch, "Where is the Truth About the Rohna?" unpublished essay, 1.
33. Wells Report to British Shipping Casualties Section, Trade Division, 17 December 1943, Admiralty, PRO.
34. Hand interview.
35. Finch to Fortune.
36. Simon Muchnick, letter to the author, 23 May 1994.
37. John Paskowski, letter to the author, 21 February 1994.
38. Mason letter.
39. Gordon, "Thankful Survivor."
40. Schoenacker diary.
41. Bronstein, "Report and Critique," 3–7; AG 704 DEAD, 5 May 1944, National Archives.
42. Phythian letter.
43. Bronstein, "Report and Critique," 9–10.

44. Harry Cullings, letter to the author, March 1995.
45. Brewer, "Sinking," 5.
46. Fievet, "Secret Disaster," 30–31. Fallon is interred in the U.S. cemetery in Tunis, North Africa.
47. Ibid., 32.
48. John Fievet interview, 28 December 1994, Birmingham, Alabama.
49. Suchan, "Voyage," 24; T. J. Murphy, Report on the Sinking of the *Rohna*, National Archives, Washington, D.C.

Chapter 5: The End of the *Rohna*

1. Dochtermann, "Angriff," 9.
2. Ibid.
3. Ibid, 10.
4. Ibid.
5. Ibid., 11.
6. Ibid., 11–12.
7. Ibid., 11–18.
8. HMS *Atherstone* Report.
9. Don Zirkle to Ed Holm, 10 November 1994, *American History Archives;* William C. Chambliss, "Recipe For Survival," *Collier's* (25 March 1944), 22.
10. Brewer, "Sinking," 7.
11. Miles letter.
12. Suchan, "Voyage," 24.
13. Phythian letter.
14. Aaron Weber, letter to the author, 26 May 1994.
15. Lacy letter.
16. Roy Jacobsen, letter to the author, n.d., 1994.
17. Boylan letter.
18. Quick letter.
19. Fievet, "The Untold Story," 11.
20. Cunigan interview.
21. Philip Anwyl, "Report on the Sinking of the *Rohna*," AG 704, National Archives.
22. Hunter letter.
23. Peach letter.
24. Loper letter.
25. Breedlove letter.
26. Spain letter.
27. Ibid.

28. Phythian letter.
29. Peach letter.
30. Clancy letter.
31. Finch to Fortune.
32. Gibson letter.
33. Finch to Fortune.
34. Boone letter.
35. Breedlove letter.
36. Jacobsen letter.
37. Caskey letter.
38. McCullough tape; Lester Rummell, letter to the author, 5 March 1995.

Chapter 6: "Only" Twenty Miles from Land

1. Hunter letter.
2. Thomas Hollimon, letter to the author, 11 February 1994.
3. Bronstein, "Report and Critique," 9–11.
4. Kroog letter.
5. Ibid.
6. Quick letter.
7. Loper letter.
8. Peach letter.
9. Ibid.
10. Ibid.
11. Jacobsen letter.
12. Boone letter.
13. Muchnick letter.
14. Jake Shimp, letter to the author, 12 March 1994.
15. Jackson, "World War Two Memoirs," 29–31.
16. Tom Merker, letter to the author, 20 September 1994.
17. Gibson letter.
18. Ken Fatton, letter to the author, 5 May 1994.
19. James Pope interview (telephone), January 1995.
20. Clancy letter.
21. Ibid.
22. Ibid.
23. Quick letter.
24. Edward Ashley, letter to the author, 26 April 1994.
25. Buckler letter.
26. Breedlove, "Sinking," 4–6; Fievet, "Secret Disaster," 29.

27. Ibid.
28. Brewer, "The Sinking," 3; Brewer interview; Lachtman, "Secret."
29. Ibid.
30. Mel Assagai, "Death Missile is Well Remembered," *Sacramento Bee,* 9 November 1976; Ernest Goen, letter to the author, n.d., 1994.
31. Ferguson letter.
32. Smith, "Memories," 7–9.
33. Ibid.
34. Inks letter.
35. Finch, "The Rohna"; Finch letter.
36. Ibid.
37. Lacy letter.
38. Horton, "Diary."

Chapter 7: To the Rescue

1. *History of USS* Pioneer (AM 105), Washington, D.C., Office of Naval Records and History, Ships' History Branch, Navy Department, U.S. Naval Yard, Washington, D.C.
2. Rogers letter.
3. "Describe the Rescue," n.d., unpublished essay, 1; USS *Pioneer* Report, 26 November 1943, National Archives.
4. Ibid.
5. Ibid.
6. Ibid.
7. Horton, "Diary."
8. Diehl tape.
9. Schoenacker letter.
10. Ferguson letter.
11. Peach letter.
12. Ibid.
13. Vickie Todd, letter to the author, n.d., 1995.
14. Peach letter.
15. Miles letter.
16. Rogers letter.
17. Caskey letter.
18. Suchan, "Voyage," 29–30.
19. Bronstein, "Report and Critique," 7.
20. McKee letter.
21. Bailey letter.

22. Smith, "Memories," 5–7.
23. Ibid.
24. Hand interview.
25. Finch, "The Rohna," 3–5.
26. Childress letter.
27. John Canney to Clyde Bellomy, 31 January 1994. From the Bellomy collection.
28. Cunigan interview.
29. Epifano letter.
30. Ed Linville, "Rohna—As I Remember It," 22 February 1994. From the Linville collection.
31. Rogers letter.
32. Clyde Bellomy, "A Part of My Story—The Sinking of the H.M.S. Rohna Day After Thanksgiving Day, Nov. 26, 1943," undated, unpublished essay. From the Bellomy collection.
33. Rogers letter.
34. Ibid. In a postscript to his letter to the author, Rogers exclaimed: "I could go on and on about our crew. Please just take my word. They were the *best!*"
35. Zirkle to Holm; Zirkle, "Report on the *Rohna,*" n.d., 1–10.
36. Ibid.
37. Zielinski Report, AG 704, National Archives.
38. Fievet, "The Untold Story," 12.
39. Inks letter.
40. HMS *Atherstone* Report.
41. Jackson, "World War Two Memoirs," 30–31.
42. Ibid.
43. Brewer interview, Ft. Scott; Brewer, "The Sinking," 3; Lachtman, "Secret."
44. Boone letter.
45. Hunter letter.
46. Mason letter.
47. Charles Crenshaw Report, AG 704, National Archives.
48. Robert D. Kruidenier Report, AG 704, National Archives.
49. *Clan Campbell* Report, November 1943, Admiralty, PRO.
50. Frolich Report, AG 704, National Archives.
51. Report, 14 January 1944, AG Files, National Archives.
52. HMS *Pelican* Report, December 1943, Admiralty, PRO.

Chapter 8: Phillipeville and Beyond

1. Dochtermann, "Angriff," 12–13.
2. Ibid.

3. Ibid.
4. Inks letter.
5. Fievet, "The Untold Story," 14.
6. Diehl tape.
7. Ibid.
8. Caskey letter.
9. Breedlove, "Sinking," 6.
10. Caskey letter.
11. Ibid.
12. Clancy letter.
13. Ibid.
14. Schoenacker letter.
15. Smith, "Memories," 10.
16. John Fievet, letter to the author, 28 February 1995.
17. Smith, "Memories," 10–11.
18. Kroog letter.
19. Ibid.
20. Horton, "Diary"; Horton letter.
21. Kroog letter; Caskey letter.
22. 853rd unit history, 6.
23. Ibid.
24. Lacy letter.
25. His diary did not say whether he landed at Bougie, or whether he landed somewhere else and then was driven to Bougie.
26. Jackson, "World War Two Memories," 31.
27. AG 704 DEAD, 5 May 1944.
28. McCarthy, "The Fiery Birth," 38–39.
29. Ibid.
30. Headquarters Depot, Bone, Cable 663 to Admiralty, Admiralty, PRO.
31. Report, "Discovery of Dead Military Personnel," 18 January 1944, AG Files, National Archives.
32. AG 704, National Archives.
33. Colonel Randolph Shaw, "Propriety of Action Under Public Law 490 as Proposed to Casualty Branch Determination," to General Benedict, 12 May 1944, AG, National Archives.
34. AG 704, National Archives.
35. Army Losses at Sea," *WASC Bulletin*, 14 June 1945. *Brassy's Naval Annual*, 44, gives different statistics.
36. Dochtermann, "Angriff," 13–19.
37. Ibid.
38. Ibid.

39. Ibid.
40. Ibid.
41. Ibid.
42. AG 704, 29 January 1944, National Archives.
43. Lucile Cherry, letter to the author, 30 May 1994.
44. Bailey letter.
45. Don Zirkle, letter to the author, February 1995.
46. Boone letter; McCullough tape.
47. Smith, "Memories," 10.
48. Childress letter.
49. Ibid.
50. Smith, "Memories," 10.
51. Ibid.
52. Ibid.
53. Caskey letter.
54. Brewer, "Sinking," 4–6.
55. Phythian letter.
56. Miles letter.
57. Jackson, "World War Two Memoirs," 34.
58. Ibid.
59. Brewer, Fort Scott interview.
60. Smith, "Memories," 11.
61. Miles letter, 4.
62. Jackson, "World War Two Memoirs," 31–33.
63. Ibid.
64. Clancy letter.
65. Caskey letter.
66. The author thanks James Brown, Eugene's son, of North Canton, Ohio, for this information.
67. Aunt Ida to Milford Bowden. The author thanks J. Evans of Calabash, North Carolina, for this information.
68. Angeline Casilio, letter to the author, 1 March 1995.
69. Miles letter, 4.
70. Ibid.
71. Finch to Wayne Dana, 16 September 1993.
72. Smith, "Memories," 12.
73. Report, Admiralty 199, PRO.
74. Caskey letter.
75. Bill Hofmann, letter to the author, 20 February 1995.
76. McCullough tape.

Chapter 9: Welcome the Travelers Home

1. Dochtermann, "Angriff," 19.
2. *Archiv der Gegenwart* XIII (1943), 6182. There is a copy of this publication in the library of Detmold, Germany.
3. Ibid.
4. Admiral Tagert, "Geleitzugkatastrophen," *Lippische Staatszeitung*, Detmold, Germany, 30 November 1943, 182.
5. Ibid.
6. James S. Thompson, letter to the author, 7 March 1995.
7. Ibid. Also Jay Reeves, "Local Man Pushing to get Story Told of WWII Sinking of Ship He was on," *Birmingham News*, 11 November 1993.
8. Fievet, "Secret Disaster," 27.
9. Penny Sward Tilley, letter to the author, 16 March 1995.
10. AG 201, 21 December 1943, National Archives.
11. AG 201, 27 March 1944, National Archives. The author thanks Mrs. Lola Buchi of Salt Lake City, Utah, for sending material about PFC Douglas Nelson.
12. *New York Times*, 18 February 1944.
13. Ibid.
14. Ibid.
15. Moak, "One Man."
16. AG 704, 26 January 1944, National Archives.
17. Ibid.
18. AG 704 DEAD, 1 March 1944, National Archives.
19. Report to Quartermaster General, 10 September 1948, AG 9107, National Archives.
20. Report, "Final Determination," 1 July 1949, AG, National Archives.
21. Joel L. Felz to Fred J. Cyr, 19 September 1986, American Battle Monuments Commission.
22. Phythian letter.
23. Andy Kalyan, letter to the author, 7 March 1995.
24. Phythian letter. See also Wesley Frank Craven and James Lea Cate (eds.), *The Army Air Forces in World War II. The Pacific: Guadalcanal to Saipan August 1942 to July 1944* (Washington, D.C.: Office of Air Force History, 1983), 465, 484–485, 492–493, 513–514.
25. Zirkle letter.
26. Phythian letter.
27. Arthur Meyer, letter to the author, 10 March 1995.
28. Eugene Piquard diary. Also, letter to the author, n.d., 1994. Another homeward bound vessel, the USS *General A. W. Greely*, also held a memorial for

the *Rohna*. Out in the North Atlantic on Thanksgiving Day, 29 November 1945, the crew's Moment of Memorial read: "On Thanksgiving Day, two years ago, the Rhona [sic] was sunk with the largest loss of American lives in the War. Men here today were among the survivors."

29. 853rd unit history, 14.
30. Gail A. Olson, *Scars and Stripes: Healing The Wounds of the War* (Bradenton, Florida: Human Services Institute, 1992), 41, 125, 135, 140–141.
31. Hunter letter.
32. Smith letter.
33. Hooks, "The Rohna Story."
34. Mitchell Landsberg, "Old Ghosts Starting to Haunt Some WWII Vets," *Courier Journal* (Louisville, Kentucky), 6 August 1995.
35. Ibid.
36. Ibid.
37. Quick letter, 24 June 1994.
38. McCullough tape.
39. Andrew Fetsko, letter to the author, 9 March 1995.
40. Dochtermann letter.
41. Hans Dochtermann interview, Frankfurt, Germany, 2 October 1995.
42. Workman, "Every Soldier."
43. Charles Osgood, Radiocast, CBS, 11 November 1993.

Bibliography

Original Documents

853rd Engineer Aviation Battalion, Unit History.

Bellomy, Clyde L. "A Part of My Story." From the Bellomy collection.

——. United States Ship USS *Pioneer* certificate.

Clounts, James G. Letter to Ernie and Jane, 1 July 1989.

Department of Army, quartermaster general. Brig. Gen. B. E. Kendall to Ruba J. Sward, Iowa, 20 March 1961.

Historical Section, Admiralty, to James G. Clonts*, 9 November 1961. From the Clounts collection.

History of USS Pioneer. Washington, D.C.: Ships' Histories Branch, U.S. Navy, n.d., unpublished.

National Archives. AG Files 471.6, *Rohna;* 704 (*Rohna*) 25 December 1943, 26 January 1944, 18 January 1944; "Determination of Status of Casualties," 29 January 1944; DEAD, 5 May 1944; Letter from F. E. Kent to adjutant general, Washington, D.C., 25 January 1946; Army Transportation Files, 569.14, *Rohna,* U.S. War Department, adjutant general; Maj. Gen. Edward F. Witsell to Edna Geher, 3 May 1946; Bronstein, Meyer.* "Report and Critique on Sinking of the HMT *Rohna,*" 17 May 1949, to chief of transportation, Department of the Army, Washington, D.C.,

1–11; Intelligence Report, Navy Department, 6, 10 December 1943; map
of area searched for survivors of the HMT *Rohna;* Shaw, Randolph.
"Propriety of Action under Public Law 490 as Proposed by Casualty
Branch Determination," 12 May 1944; USS *Pioneer* Action Report, 26
November 1943; USS *Pioneer* Reports, 25–27 November 1943; *Pioneer*
Background Information, n.d., unpublished pamphlet; USS *Portent* Report,
"Anti-Aircraft Action by Surface Ships," 28 November 1943; War Depart-
ment, "Incoming Message," 28 November 1943; OPD569.14, 27 Decem-
ber 1943; War Department, "Incoming Message," 27 December 1943;
Mallon, E. L. Letter to assistant chief of staff for operations, 5 January 1944.
Parmentier, Albert. Diary. Alabama.
Piquard, Eugene E. Diary. Piquard collection.
Public Records Office (PRO) collection. Kew, London: Admiralty file number
1.12134, 12129, 12130; Admiralty file number 199.103, 243, 464, 731,
976, 1175, 1178, 1181, 1783, 2107, 2137, 2151, 2152; Air. 27.
PRO. Ministry of Defense, Kew, London: Summary of Service for HMS
Atherstone, October 1979; "Loss of the Troopship Rohna," July 1978.
"Army Losses at Sea." *WASC Bulletin.* 14 June 1945.

Unpublished Works

Brewer, Robert.* "The Sinking of the Rohna." Undated.
Di Folco, Louis. "The Pioneer Comes Through—Sung to the Tune of Casey
Jones." 1943. Used with permission.
Dochtermann, Hans. "Angriff auf den US Geleitzug KMF 26 vor der Bucht von
Bougie." 14 July 1992.
Fievet, John P. "HMT Rohna—The Untold Story" (received by author 11
November 1993). Undated.
Finch, Charles. "The Truth about the *Rohna.*" Undated.
———. "The *Rohna.*" Undated.
———. "The *Rohna,* Why the Secret?" Undated.
———. "Missiles Are Not New." Undated.
———. "Where is the Truth about the Rohna?" Undated.
Jones, Harrell. "The Angel of the Sea." Poem in letter to the author. 1994, 1995.
Used with permission.
Kuberski, Hank.* "World War II's Best Kept Secret: The Sinking of the HMT
Rohna, November 26, 1943; With the Loss of 1015 Men; The British
Convoy, KMF 26. Undated, unpublished essay.
"Memorial Service for Those Who Lost Their Lives Aboard the HMT *Rohna,*"
26 November 1943. Gatlinburg, Tennessee, 29 September 1993.

Smith, John. "Memories Recalled 50 Years After the HMT *Rohna* Disaster, November 26, 1943." 1993.

Wright, Ron. "Description of the Rescue." Undated.

Books, Journal Articles, and Broadcasts

Albrecht, Brian E. "A Devastating First: Witness Recounts the *Rohna*'s Death by Guided Missile." *Plain Dealer* (Cleveland, Ohio), 23 May 1993.

Assagai, Mel. "Death Missile is Well Remembered." *Sacramento Bee,* 9 November 1976.

Balloch, Jim. "Secrecy Remains on World War II Incident." *Knoxville News Sentinel,* 30 November 1993.

Banigan, John. "If You Are Torpedoed." *Science Digest* (6 June 1943): 73–76.

Barkley, Meredith. "Disaster: Secrecy Shrouds Ship." *Ledger,* September 1993.

———. "Big Secret: 50 Years after Disaster Mystery Still Surrounds Bombing of HMS Rohna." *Ledger,* 17 October 1993 (story of Toby Almond*, Eden, North Carolina).

Beetham, George, Jr. "50 Years Later, Vet Give Thanks for Missing Boat." *Review* (Hila, Pennsylvania), 1, 11.

Canney, John. "HMT Rohna Survivors Hold 50th Reunion." *CBIVA Sound-Off* (Winter 1994): 49. From the Canney collection.

Craven, Wesley Frank, and James Lea Cate (eds.). *The Army Air Forces in World War II.* Vol. 4 (Washington, D.C.: Office of Air Force History, 1983).

Chambliss, William C. "Recipe for Survival." *Collier's,* 17 March 1944, 22.

Deering, Sally. "World War II Survivor Marks 50th." *Jersey Journal,* 28 October 1993.

Daily Mirror (London), 24 June 1987.

Eubank, Keith. *Summit at Tehran* (New York: William Morrow, 1985).

Feller, Jane. "Surviving Shipmates Plan 50-Year Reunion." *Lassen County Times* (Susanville, California), 3 August 1993.

Fievet, John P. "World War II's Secret Disaster." *American History* 29(3) (August 1994): 24–35.

Fortune, Don. "Sinking of the Rohna." *VFW Magazine* (October 1993): 42.

———. "It's Time—After 50 Years—To Recognize the Sinking of the *Rohna.*" *San Francisco Examiner,* 25 July 1993.

Gordon, William. "Thankful Survivor," *Newark Star-Ledger,* 24 November 1993.

Green, William. *War Planes of the Third Reich* (New York: Galahad Books, 1967).

Guided Bomb. Television documentary (New York: Video Ordnance, 1993).

Hewitt, Albertus.* "A Troopship Sinks." *Gateway* (Pennsylvania) Autumn 1944, 5–6.

Hocking, Charles. *Dictionary of Disasters at Sea during the Age of Steam* (London: Lloyds, 1969).

Hogg, I.V. *German Secret Weapons of World War II* (New York: Arco Publishing, 1970).

Hooks, Thomas J. "The *Rohna* Story." *Ex-CBI Roundup* (July 1986): 6–10.

Horst, Boog. *Die Deutsche Luftwaffenfurung, 1935–1945* (Stuttgart: Deutsche Verlag-Anstalt, 1982).

Huntington, Tom. "V-2: The Long Shadow." *Air & Space* (February/March 1993): 81–90.

Jackson, Carlton. *A Social History of the Scotch-Irish* (Lanham, Maryland: Madison Books, 1993).

Jackson, Ulys*. "My World War Two Memoirs." In Mrs. Ulys Jackson, *David and Anney (Bowen) Jackson in Tennessee and Arkansas; Some Ancestors and Descendants* (Point Lookout, Missouri: The School of the Ozarks Press, 1977).

Kester, Kyra. *The Historical Dimensions and Social Implications of Military Psychology and Veteran Counseling in the United States, 1860–1989.* Ph.D. dissertation, University of Washington, 1992.

Lord, Walter. *A Night to Remember* (New York: Holt, 1955).

Lachtman, Howard. "Secret." *Stockton (California) Record*, 22 July 1993.

Landsberg, Mitchell. "Old Ghosts Starting to Haunt Some WWII Vets." *Courier-Journal* (Louisville, Kentucky), 6 August 1995.

McCarthy, Dan B. "The Fiery Birth of Missile Warfare," *VFW Magazine* (November 1967): 21, 38–39.

Mayle, Paul D. *Eureka Summit: Agreeement in Principle and the Big Three at Tehran, 1943* (Newark, Delaware: University of Delaware, 1987).

Mehner, Kurt. *Die Geheimen Tagesberichte Der Deutschen Wehrmachtfurung im Zweiten Weltkrieg 1939–1945* (Osnabruck, Germany: Biblio Verlag, 1988).

Moak, David L. "One Man Has Never Forgotten." *Herald Dispatch* (West Virgina), 26 November 1993.

Molesworth, Carl. *Wing to Wing: Air Combat in China 1943–1945* (New York: Orion Books, 1990).

"More than 1,000 U.S. Soldiers Died, But History Overlooks the HMT *Rohna*." *Post-Tribune* (Jefferson City, Missouri), 11 November 1993.

Neufeld, Michael J. *The Rocket and the Reich: Peenemunde and the Coming of the Ballistic Missile Era* (New York: Free Press, 1995).

New York Times, 18 February 1944.

Nowarra, Heinz J. *Die Deutsche Luftrustung 1933–1945* (Koblenz, Germany: Bernard & Graefe Verlag, 1993).

Olson, Gail A. *Scars and Stripes: Healing the Wounds of the War* (Bradenton, Florida: Human Services Institute, 1992).

"1,000 Yanks Die as Troopship Sinks," *Birmingham (Alabama) Age-Herald*, 18 February 1944.

Osgood, Charles. "Forgotten Soldiers." CBS radio broadcast, 11 November 1993.

Anonymous. "The *Rohna*." Poem.

Anonymous. "The Sinking of the *Rohna*." Poem.

Quick, John. *Dictionary of Weapons and Military Terms* (New York: McGraw-Hill, 1973).

Reeves, Jay. "Local Man Pushing to Get Story Told of World War II Sinking of Ship He Was on." *Birmingham News*, 11 November 1993.

Rogers, H. C. B. *Troopships and Their History* (London: Seely Services, 1963).

Roskill, S. W. *The War at Sea 1939–1945.* Vol. 3: "The Offensive," part 1: June 1943–May 31, 1944 (London: Her Majesty's Stationery Office, 1960).

St. George Saunders, Hilary. *Valiant Voyaging* (London: Faber and Faber, 1948).

Shaw, James L. "Rajula . . . A Liner Unsung But Not Forgotten." *Ships Monthly* (June 1980): 27–28.

Sikora, Frank. "Survivor Recalls Escape from Missile Attack." *Birmingham News*, 9 November 1992.

Smith, J. R., and Kay, Anthony L. *German Aircraft of the Second World War* (Baltimore, Maryland: The Nautical and Aviation Publishing Company of America, 1972).

Strecker, Edward A., and Appel, Kenneth E. *Psychiatry in Modern Warfare* (New York: MacMillan Co., 1945).

Suchan, Tom. "Voyage of Death." *Beacon* (Akron, Ohio), 18 November 1973, 5–8; 9–10; 24–25.

Tagert, D. "Geleitzugkatastrophen." *Lippische Staatszeitung* (Detmold, Germany), 30 November 1943.

"Thanksgiving Memory Haunts Local Vet." *Derrick* (Pittsburgh, Pennsylvania), 24 November 1993.

Toland, John. *Infamy: Pearl Harbor And Its Aftermath* (New York: Doubleday, 1982).

"Voyage on the Karoa: 252 Port Co.: A Short History." *Ex-CBI Roundup* (November 1986): 4–5.

Wegmann, Gunter. *Das Oberkommando der Wehrmacht Gibt Bekannt* (Osnabruck, Germany: Biblio Verlag, 1982).

Workman, Will. "Every Soldier Has a Story." *Record* (Rock Hill, New York), 21 November 1993.

Letters and Tapes (addressed to the author, unless otherwise noted)

Anderson, Oscar F. New York. 24 February, 21 March 1995.
Anderson, Robert. New Jersey. 29 March 1995.
Ashley, Edward L.* Virginia. 26 April 1994.
Ashley, Ronald.* Ohio. 21 April 1994.
Bailey, Clarence J.* Virginia. 5 June 1994.
Bartolotta, Louis.* Florida. 12 April 1994.
Bauer, Charles R.* New Jersey. 1994.
Bazzarre, Roy. West Virginia. 26 September 1994.
Birsa, Bruno. Pennsylvania. 1994.
Blaine, James. California. 1 March 1995.
Bleike, Dale C. Texas. 6 March 1995.
Boone, Wilmot.* Hawaii. 20 January 1994.
Borows, Arthur.* New York. 20 April 1994.
Boylan, Raymond J.* Florida. 1994.
Braid, Brenda. Birkenhead, England. 8 March 1995.
Braid, S. Liverpool, England. 10 March 1995.
Breedlove, Eugene.* Arkansas. 22 January 1994.
Brown, James. Ohio. 16 March 1995.
Brumbach, Aaron A. Pennsylvania. 26 September 1994.
Buchi, Lola. Utah. 22 March 1995.
Buckler, John.* Tyne & Wear, England. 29 June, 22 August, 20 October 1994.
Burdett, Frank. Sheffield, England. 6 March 1995.
Burke, Ed.* Massachusetts. 16 March 1994.
Burlingame, Lulu. Wisconsin. 9 March 1995.
Caldwell, George. California. 9 March 1995.
Canney, John P.* Ohio. 29 January, 24 March 1994; 19 February 1995; to Clyde
    Bellomy, 31 January 1994.
Capozzi, Tony. Indiana. 7 March 1995.
Casilio, Angeline. Pennsylvania. March 1995.
Caskey, William.* California. 3 February 1994; to Richard Buckingham, 18
    November 1993; to Charles Osgood, 29 April 1994; to Harrell Jones, 14
    December 1993.
Cherry, Russell.* North Carolina. 30 May 1994.
Chessire, Mrs. W. D. Iowa. 25 March 1995.
Childress, Parker.* Alabama. 19 January 1994.
Clancy, Charles.* Wisconsin. 15 March 1994.
Conway, Thomas.* 28 November 1994.
Coon, Harold H.* California. 2 March 1995.

Cullings, Harry.* Pennsylvania. March 1995.
Cuming, Robert N. California. 12 April 1995.
Dawes, Herb. Pennsylvania. 27 February 1994.
Davis, Jack. Ohio. March 1994.
Dettman, Fred. Georgia. 21 May 1994.
Diehl, Forrest.* Ohio. Tape to the author. 1994.
Different, Paul. Mississippi. 14 May 1994.
Dochtermann, Hans. 4 October 1992.
Dockum, Marilyn, writing about Joseph Morocco.* New York. 8 March 1994.
Drogo, Louis. New York. 2 October 1994.
Dryhurst, Evans. Maryland. 27 March 1995.
Evans, J. Ray. North Carolina. March 1995.
Epifano, Raymond.* New Jersey. No date.
Fatton, Ken.* New York. 5 May 1994.
Farmer, Janet. Stockport, England. 14 March 1995.
Felz, Joel L., Report to North African American Cemetery and Memorial, 25 November 1986. National Archives.
Ferguson, Richard.* Oregon. 14 May 1994.
Fetsko, Andrew.* Ohio. 5 May, 23 June 1994.
Fievet, John P.* Alabama. 11 November 1993.
Finch, Charles.* Texas. 24 January 1994; to Paul S. Atkins, 17 August 1993; to Wayne Dana (from Finch collection), 16 September 1993; to Don Fortune, 26 July 1993, 19 July 1994.
Finn, Robert. Pennsylvania. 31 March 1995.
Fonte, Vincent.* Connecticut. 4 March 1994.
Freeman, Charles. Mississippi. 3 October 1994.
Fugill, John T. Barnehurst, England. 12 March 1995.
Fullard, S. Newcastle on Tyne, England. March 1995.
Garrett, Milton. Kentucky. 4 March 1995.
Gerstenmaier, Charles.* Connecticut. 2 March 1995.
Gibson, J. B.* South Carolina. 16 May 1994; to Forrest Ashmead, 13 April 1990 (Gibson collection).
Glassey, John B., Jr.* New York. 24 May 1994.
Goen, Ernest.* California. 1994.
Gough, Harold.* New Jersey. 17 May 1995.
Granfield, Maurice.* Massachusetts. 24 January 1994.
Harding, John. California. 7 March 1995.
Hartner, Ted. Wisconsin. 27 March 1995.
Harvey, Alan and Gita. Tasmania, Australia. January 1995.
Hawthorne, Ed. Farnam, England. 13 March 1995.
Head, Joseph. Sunderland, England. 17 March 1995.

Heming, E. M. Lymington, England. 17 March 1995.

Heberle, Henry.* Pennslyvania. 8 March 1995.

Hoffman, Bill.* Florida. 20, 21 February 1995.

Hollimon, Thomas G.* Louisiana. 11 February 1994.

Horton, Ernest.* Texas. 6 May 1994; to Charlotte and James, 11 June 1989; Horton, "Excerpts from the Diary," n.d., unpublished.

Hudec, William.* Pennsylvania. 1994.

Hunter, Dana.* Maine. 3 May 1994.

Inks, Camdon.* Pennsylvania. 23 May 1994.

Ives, Irving. To Carl Schoenacker.* New York. 9 January 1951.

Jackson, Mrs. James (Betty). Ohio. 1 June 1995.

Jacobsen, Roy.* New Jersey. 1994.

Johnson, Phillip E. Florida. March 1995.

Johnston, W. H. Indiana. 12 May 1994.

Jordan, J. Exeter, England. 9 March 1995.

Joshi, Madhavrao D. Bombay, India. 8 January 1995.

Kadis, A. M. Ohio. 25 January 1994.

Kalyan, Andrew.* Connecticut. 7, 13 March 1995; to Harrell Jones, 10 February 1994.

Kroog, Theodore.* New York. 9 March 1994.

Lacy, James.* Kansas. 1994.

Lewis, Mike. Minnesota. 2 February 1995.

Linville, Ed. "Rohna—As I Remember It" (letter). 22 February 1994.

Livingston, Ben.* Illinois. March 1995.

Loper, James.* Georgia. 31 December 1994; to John Fievet, May, 18 June, August 1994, 13 January 1995.

Mallory, Maurice.* New York. 27 May 1994.

Mason, Wallace J.* North Carolina. 31 August 1994.

Matthews, Bill.* South Carolina. 24 May 1994.

McCullough, William E. South Carolina. 10 March 1995; tape to author, March 1995.

McKee, Bill.* South Carolina. 22 May 1994.

Maryeski, Joseph. Connecticut. 16 March 1995.

Merker, Tom.* Florida. 20 September 1994.

Meyer, Arthur.* Iowa. 10 March 1995.

Miles, Herald.* California. 18 May 1994.

Miller, John. New York. 29 September 1994.

Moro, Edna Geher. New York. 6 March 1995; to Mrs. John P. Canney, 24 March 1994.

Muchnick, Simon.* Missouri. 23 May 1994.

Munger, Pat. Nevada. 10 March 1995.

Neufeld, Michael J. Washington, D.C. 21 June 1994.

O'Haver, Barbara. Arizona. 2 March 1995.

Palmer, F. Bognore Regis, England. 4 March 1995.

Panion, Fred.* Montana. 18 May 1995.

Paskowski, John.* Michigan. 21, 24 February 1994.

Peach, Richard.* Pennsylvania. 16 March 1994.

Percle, Corbett J.* Louisiana. 12 May 1994.

Phythian, Richard.* Michigan. 10 May 1994.

Pickering, H. Churchdown, England. 8 March 1995.

Quick, William C.* New York. 24 June 1994.

Quilty, William T. Kentucky. 7 March 1995.

Randall, T. A. Twickenham, England. 14 March 1995.

Randis, Walter.* Pennsylvania. March 1995.

Rees, Louis. Arizona. March 1995.

Rhines, Milford.* Connecticut. 14 February 1994.

Rice, Herman.* Ohio. 11 March 1995.

Rogers, John. North Carolina. 3 March 1995.

Rogers, LeRoy. Georgia. 22 June, 23 September 1994.

Rosseau, John.* Massachusetts. 23 February 1995.

Rummel, Lester. Arkansas. 5 March 1995.

Runk, Douglas J. Texas. 10, 13 March 1995.

Sanyal, M. K. Calcutta, India. 28 December 1994.

Sagan, Edwin. Connecticut. 8 May 1995.

Sandoval, Vincente.* Texas. 12 May 1994.

Schoenacker, Carl.* New York. 20, 30 June 1994, 19 February 1995; to Harrell
    Jones, 10 January 1994.

Shimp, Jake.* South Dakota. 12 March 1994; to "Jay and Lois," 3 March 1992.

Schmitt, William. Nebraska. 10 March 1995.

Shuey, Chester. Florida. 14 March 1995.

Sinare, Anthony. Florida. 5 May 1994.

Skold, Elmer A. Missouri. 1994.

Smutny, Ludvik. Nebraska. 8 February 1995.

Snyder, Louie. Idaho. 19 May 1995.

Spain, Jasper L. Georgia. 13 March 1995.

Stites, Everett. Ohio. 14 March 1995.

Stout, Marshall.* New York. 5 June 1994.

Straight, Keith B. Wisconsin. 13 March 1995.

Straley, Russ. Pennsylvania. 6 March 1995.

Strohmeyer, Robert. Kansas. 9 March 1995.

Sullivan, J. Don. Texas. 7 March 1995.

Taylor, Francis M. California. 9 March 1995.

Taylor, Jacob.* Pennsylvania. 21 March 1995.
Tietz, Dieter. Alabama. 23 June 1994.
Tilley, Penny (Sward). Texas. 16 March 1995.
Thompson, James S. Tyne & Wear, England. 7 March 1995.
Turner, Austin. California, 1 May 1995.
Turner, William H. Pennsylvania. April 1995.
Tylek, Matthew. Florida. 14 March 1995.
Usher, Richard. New York. 15 March 1995; to James Clonts*, 3 January 1988.
Van Ausdall, Robert Loren. Illinois. 3 March 1995.
Vangi, John.* New Jersey. March 1995.
Walters, John. Georgia. 3 March 1995.
Weber, Aaron.* Pennsylvania. 26 May 1994.
Wehrle, Charles. Ohio. 7 March 1995.
Weiss, Lothar. Detmold, Germany. 3 August 1994.
Wood, Joan. Plymouth, England. 15 March 1995.
Ziglar, E. J. Illinois. 1 April 1995.
Zirkle, Don.* Nevada. March 1995; letter to Ed Holm, 10 November 1994,
    "Report on the Rohna," 1–13.

Interviews (interviewed by the author, unless otherwise noted)

Brewer, Robert.* Interviewed by Larry Morrison. Shaw Air Force Base, Illinois.
    4 October 1983.
Cunigan, Sam. Auburn, Kentucky. 20 November 1994.
Dochtermann, Hans. Frankfurt, Germany. 2 October 1995.
Hand, R. J.* Texas. Telephone interview. January 1995.
Levine, Saul.* New York. Telephone interview. December 1994.
Pope, James.* North Carolina. Telephone interview. 1994.
Shelton, Charles.* Russellville, Kentucky. 10 December 1994.

*Indicates *Rohna* survivor.

Index

Lacy, James, 97, 126, 169
Lake Ishamalia, 139
Lambert Cadwalader, 9
lascars, 2, 15, 18, 32, 56, 64; and
 Rohna lifeboats, 67–68, 79, 86,
 91, 94, 139, 147
Leide, Reinhard, 21
LeMay, Curtis, 150
Lenox, Tenn., 9
Le Sabala, 35
Lewis, Donald, 169
Lewis, Ted, 12
Linville, Ed, 110, 111
Loper, James, 12, 17, 49, 50, 79, 87
Luftflotte, 22
Luftwaffe, 19, 20, 21, 122, 129, 130

Mae West life preservers, 64, 79
Manhard, Monfred, 22
Marine Robin, 153
Marnix Van St. Aldegonde, 3
Mason, Wallace, 6, 61, 70, 81, 118,
 119, 167
Matschke, H., 75
Mayle, Paul, 8, 174
McCullough, William, 36, 48
McKee, Bill, 63, 106, 107
Mediterranean Sea, xiv, 3, 8, 9, 12, 15,
 18, 23, 25, 29, 30, 35, 62, 68, 71,
 74, 75, 76, 77, 78, 82, 99, 108, 125,
 127, 137, 142, 146, 148, 153
Meetha, Serang Bhowan, 67
Memorial Division Identification
 Branch, 148
Merignac, France, 74, 76, 121
Merker, Tom, 90, 150
"Merrill's Marauders," 150
Mers El Khebir, Algeria, 101
Meyer, Arthur, 153
Miaoules, 25
Miles, Herald, 61, 77, 105, 168
Mindful, 25, 83, 99, 113; rescuing
 survivors, 116–18, 120, 122

Mons, R., 22, 36, 122
Montpelier, France, 76
Mont Viso, 3
Muchnick, Simon, 69, 89, 167
Murphy, T. J. (Capt. of the *Rohna*),
 13–14, 15, 28, 31, 32, 37, 43, 46,
 48, 56, 60, 65, 72, 80, 82, 92, 98

Neary, Thomas, 133
Nelson, Lola A., 144
"Neville," the goat, 13–14, 56
Newcastle upon Tyne, 3
News blackouts, 141–46
New York Times, 144, 146
Nicholas Gilman, 10
Nivose, 3
NOK (Next of Kin), 170
Normandy, 3, 168
North Africa, 3, 8, 10, 11, 24, 25, 35,
 102, 118, 119, 120, 122, 127, 133,
 134, 135, 144, 148

Oerlikon cannons, 4
Operation Overlord, 8
Operation Torch, 3, 126
Oran, Algeria, 3, 9, 11, 12, 15, 16, 28,
 62, 68, 101, 127, 139
Orion, 34, 39
Osgood, Charles, xvi, 157, 170

Palestine, 127
paravane device, 46
Paskowski, John, 70
Peach, Richard, xv, xvi, 50, 51, 57,
 58, 63, 79, 80, 81, 87, 88, 104,
 105, 167
Peenemunde, Germany, 21
Peiser, Harold, 28
Pelican, 25, 114, 119
Phillipeville, Algeria, 113, 119, 120,
 122, 123, 124, 126, 129, 133, 134
Phythian, Richard, 31, 70, 78, 80,
 150, 153